the
red hot
chile sauce
book

the red hot chile sauce book

more than **100** fabulously fiery sauces for chile fans

Dan May

photography by Peter Cassidy

RYLAND PETERS & SMALL
LONDON • NEW YORK

Senior Designer Barbara Zuñiga
Commissioning Editor Céline Hughes
Production Controller Gary Hayes
Art Director Leslie Harrington
Editorial Director Julia Charles

Food Stylist Lizzie Harris
Prop Stylist Róisín Nield
Indexer Hilary Bird

First published in 2013 by
Ryland Peters & Small
20–21 Jockey's Fields
London WC1R 4BW
and
519 Broadway, 5th Floor
New York, NY 10012
www.rylandpeters.com

10 9 8 7 6 5 4 3 2 1

Text © Dan May 2013
Design and photographs
© Ryland Peters & Small 2013

Printed in China

UK ISBN: 978 1 84975 436 1
US ISBN: 978 1 84975 455 2

A CIP record for this book is available from
the British Library.

A CIP record for this book is available from
the Library of Congress.

NOTES

- The recipes in this book are given in both metric and imperial measurements. However, the spellings are primarily British and this includes all terminology relating to chilli peppers. British "chilli" and "chillies" are used where Americans would use "chile", "chili" and "chiles".
- All spoon measurements are level unless otherwise specified.
- All herbs are fresh unless otherwise specified.
- All eggs are medium (UK) or large (US) unless otherwise specified. Uncooked or partially cooked eggs should not be served to the very young, the very old, those with compromised immune systems, or to pregnant women.
- When a recipe calls for the grated zest of citrus fruit, buy unwaxed fruit and wash well before use. If you can only find treated fruit, scrub well in warm soapy water and rinse before using.
- Ovens should be preheated to the specified temperature. Recipes in this book were tested using a regular oven. If using a fan/convection oven, follow the manufacturer's instructions for adjusting temperatures.
- Sterilize preserving jars before use. Wash them in hot, soapy water and rinse in boiling water. Place in a large saucepan and then cover with hot water. With the lid on, bring the water to the boil and continue boiling for 15 minutes. Turn off the heat, then leave the jars in the hot water until just before they are to be filled. Invert the jars onto clean kitchen paper to dry. Sterilize the lids for 5 minutes, by boiling, or according to the manufacturer's instructions. Jars should be filled and sealed while they are still hot.

contents

Introduction 6

Mexico & South America 10

Africa 28

Caribbean 50

Mediterranean 66

USA 84

India 100

South-East Asia 118

China & Japan 138

Suppliers & Stockists 156

Index 158

Acknowledgments 160

Introduction

When I wrote *The Red Hot Chilli Cookbook* it gave me the wonderful opportunity to share some of the things I have always loved to cook. Their roots were in places I had visited and things I had tasted but their unifying thread was that they had been gathered almost by chance over many years – and of course contained lots of chilli!

This book was slightly different; many of the recipes were ones I have, in principle, known for years and have loved to make but as I began to look at the ingredients and the way people cooked around the world I realized that each culture's approach to their food needed to be considered before I could really understand the processes and skills that make each recipe special. The traditional techniques that can so often be replaced with modern kitchen conveniences had genuine value in the flavour and consistency of the finished paste or sauce. Each one is special because it represents a particular flavour combination or way of doing things that is often unique to a small geographic area. Although this book is undoubtedly about chillies and the love of chillies it is also about cooking, eating and sharing and how universally important these things are no matter where you happen to live.

The inescapable fact is that food is key to our existence. The only thing we require with more regularity if we want to stay alive is water; and yet we have continued to erode its importance with our constant scrabbling to find some way of producing it more cheaply, more quickly or more conveniently as though our basic human requirement was in reality an inconvenience. I believe that something so vital and with the potential to provide so much pleasure should be afforded the time and attention befitting its role in our lives. If we look out into the wider world we see culture after culture where food is respected and dishes are made by tried and tested methods that show an understanding of the ingredients. This understanding combined with the patience required to make sometimes complex pastes and sauces illustrates the importance of food and its preparation in the regions in this book.

People often associate the decline in an interest in "real" food and an increasing love of heavily processed food with increasing wealth; this in itself seems weird but to a degree the figures back this up. We do seem to be exceptional in the way we insist that our food should be as cheap as possible, no matter what the real cost.

With the exception of the USA, people in the UK spend less as a percentage of their income (less than 8%) on food than any other comparable country in the world. If we make a direct comparison with average expenditure across other European countries we find that the UK only spends 53% or just over half the amount our European counterparts regularly spend per person on food. It is a simple fact that (for example) Indonesia which spends 43% of annual income on food has to do so because average incomes are considerably lower, but given the European example it is clear that some countries just place a higher value on the quality and freshness of their food and on paying the producers a fair price to make it for them! They also like to have a say in the way it is delivered to them – weekly food markets, butchers, online, and also via the supermarket. Food undoubtedly becomes cheaper if it is heavily processed (thus has a longer shelf life), is sourced on a huge scale and sold through a few channels. But this model does little for maintaining real choice, quality and an understanding of the food we are eating. In an effort to feed the profits of "the delivery channel" everything else involved suffers and inevitably corners are cut. In the population as a whole it inexorably leads to less fresh food, less cooking from scratch and even more worryingly, fewer of the skills required to do this being passed to the next generation; and this doesn't even begin to address the inherent health issues.

By the time I was 10, against my better judgement, I could have a pretty good stab at spaghetti Bolognese, a roast dinner or a decent curry and I was not exceptional. I recently carried out an ad-hoc survey with a group of my 10-year-old son's friends and found not a single one could cook any of these dishes or even similar, and more than half of them had never even helped to make a single meal they had eaten. To me, cooking is a life skill; it enables you to look after yourself. It is inconceivable to imagine this as less important than, for example, the ability to create a PowerPoint presentation, use social media, or drive.

Culturally it seems preparing fresh home-cooked meals is not regarded highly enough within our modern families to warrant the time or effort involved – why bother if no one appreciates it? It is interesting (or should I say impossible) to imagine say an Italian, Spanish or Greek family having no regard for the person who cooked for them or interest in the story of their food!

But it is not solely health and nutritional benefits that are gained from complete cooking – to me these are almost side issues. The real benefit comes in the social aspects of food, of taking the time to sit down and eat and talk. If I search my mind for significant days in my life, those that immediately spring forward are ones that involved cooking and eating with family and friends and the fun that ensued.

The most popular dishes of countries give us great insight into their culture, and the British willingness to adopt ideas and flavours from all over the world makes our food among the most interesting anywhere in the world. We readily accept and encourage change, which is probably what has kept our culture so alive and exciting over the past 150 years. There are few places in the world where chillies and spicy food have been so enthusiastically embraced or where the culture of eating chillies and challenging your palate reaches such extremes.

Despite the huge cultural differences between the Caribbean, the UK, Spain, South Africa, India, China, the USA and all the other regions covered in this book, there exists a unified "chilli culture" that dares itself to eat hotter and hotter food, that loves to laugh at anyone who exceeds their tolerance and loves to share their food and experiences with anyone who is interested. There is fun and experimentation, and behind it all there is more often than not a willing social interaction, collaboration and good food!

So do we use cooking as an excuse to use spices and chillies or are they the excuse to cook? I don't think it really matters; as long as the two go hand in hand we get the fun and the benefits of both; as well as hopefully preserving some pretty fantastic old recipes and learning how to use them. To paraphrase the legendary but apocryphal quote by Benjamin Franklin about beer: maybe chillies are proof that God loves us and wants us to be happy!

Noted Chillies: The Poblano which, when ripened fully and dried, is referred to as the Ancho, Chipotle, Orange Habanero, Rocoto, Pasilla, Brazilian Starfish, Aji Amarillo (pictured here), Aji Limo.

Chilli Facts and Fiction: Aztec Kings used to drink a combination of hot chocolate and crushed dried chillies to "stimulate" themselves before visiting their concubines.

Chapter One

Mexico & South America

The home of chillies. All chillies originate from the northern Amazon basin, the northern part of South America and Central America.

- The Chiltepin or Tepin chilli is commonly regarded as the oldest variety in the world. The "Mother Chilli", as it is also known, still thrives in the wilds of Northern Mexico where, despite the harsh environment, it can live and fruit for up to 20 years.

- Peru and Bolivia were the first countries to grow chillies for food and medicine. There is evidence of chilli cultivation taking place 5000–6000 years ago not only in both these countries but in Ecuador too.

- Brazil seems most likely to be the country from which chillies began to spread all over the world at the hands of Portuguese traders, beginning in 1500 when Cabral landed on the Brazilian coast.

- Most varieties of chillies thrive in this region, but South America is especially known for the *Capsicum Pubescens* (Rocoto, Locoto and Manzano), famed for their hairy leaves and stems, and *Capsicum Baccatum* species (Aji chillies – Aji Amarillo, Aji Limon), with a delicious citrusy overtone to their flavours.

- Mexico has the widest variety of chillies in commercial production and is the source of most of the world's Chipotle chillies – dried, smoked red Jalapeños, used in countless barbecue sauces and marinades.

- Our English word "chilli" is actually derived directly from the Aztec or Nahuatl language.

Ají Criollo

This is a very fine salsa recipe from Ecuador. Although "Capsicum Baccatum" chillies are the least common throughout the rest of the world, in South America (and to a certain extent Central America) they are the most prevalent. The various Ají's grow remarkably well in a greenhouse or on a windowsill. However, if you haven't grown any or can't source any, just substitute with Habanero chillies at a 50–75% ratio, as they can be considerably hotter!

4 Ají or 2–3 Habanero chillies, deseeded and chopped

a good handful of coriander/cilantro stalks and leaves, chopped

3 plump garlic cloves, chopped

juice of ½ lemon

1 small onion or shallot, finely chopped

sea salt

100 ml/scant ½ cup water

1 spring onion/scallion, chopped into 5-mm/¼-inch pieces

Put the chillies, coriander/cilantro, garlic, lemon juice and onion into mortar and pound with the pestle to combine. Season with salt and add as much of the water as required to loosen the mixture. Continue to pound until you have an even, yet textured, paste. Mix the spring onion/scallion through and serve.

I would use this: as a light, hot marinade for chicken before grilling/broiling, or as a dip for strips of barbecued beef or chicken.

Green Honey Salsa

Wild Mexican honey has a distinctive flavour and is not overly sweet, making it perfect for rounding off the flavours of this green salsa. If you can't get any fresh Poblano chillies, try to find any large, very mild chilli to use in its place.

1 large green sweet/bell pepper, deseeded and finely chopped

1 Poblano chilli, deseeded and finely chopped

1 onion, finely chopped

2 garlic cloves, crushed

4 green Jalapeño chillies, deseeded and cut into fine strips

a small handful of coriander/cilantro, finely chopped

2–3 teaspoons dark Mexican honey

a good squeeze of lime juice

1 teaspoon aged Tequila

a drizzle of olive oil

sea salt and freshly ground black pepper

Mix together all the ingredients (except the oil, and salt and pepper), cover and refrigerate for 1–2 hours before serving. Season well with salt and pepper and sprinkle with a little olive oil just before serving.

I would use this: in spicy chicken fajitas.

Classic Guacamole (opposite: top)

If you want a classic dip with a long history, then look no further than guacamole – originally made by the Aztecs in the 16th century. In its purest form, all it contains is avocado mashed with salt, but over the centuries more and more variations have been developed. This is my favourite version of the dip.

3 ripe avocados, skinned, pitted and roughly chopped

1 vine-ripened tomato, skinned, deseeded and roughly chopped

3 fresh green chillies, deseeded and finely chopped

juice of 2 small limes

a little extra virgin olive oil

2 spring onions/scallions, finely chopped

a small bunch of coriander/cilantro, finely chopped

sea salt and freshly ground black pepper

In a large bowl, mash the avocados, tomato and chillies together with the lime juice. The consistency should be chunky yet smooth – add a little olive oil to help achieve this. Add the onions and coriander/cilantro and mix well. Season with salt and pepper to taste and serve immediately.

I would use this: with tortillas to dip; on nachos; on the side of a spicy chili; or in homemade burritos.

Salsa Roja (opposite: bottom)

This is a hot salsa of charred tomato and 3 classic Mexican chillies. If you can't get fresh De Arbol and Guajillo, use dried, toast them for 2 minutes on each side, soak in a small amount of boiling water for about 20 minutes, then remove their stems and deseed them. Reserve the soaking liquid for the recipe.

2 tablespoons olive oil

1 onion, finely chopped

4–5 large plum tomatoes, halved and core removed

2–3 garlic cloves

1 teaspoon dried oregano

1 fresh Serrano or Jalapeño chilli, deseeded and chopped

3 fresh or dried De Arbol chillies, deseeded and chopped

5 fresh or dried Guajillo chillies, deseeded and chopped

a small bunch of coriander/cilantro, finely chopped

sea salt and freshly ground black pepper

Heat a heavy-based frying pan or griddle over fairly high heat. Add a little oil and fry the onion and tomatoes hard until they begin to blacken (about 7–11 minutes), but stir as required to prevent burning. Add the garlic and cook for a further 3–4 minutes.

Transfer the contents of the pan to a food processor with the oregano and chillies. Add the remaining oil as you blend (and the liquid you soaked the chillies in, if you used dried) until you have a smooth and even paste. Season to taste with salt and pepper, then add the coriander/cilantro and briefly blend again to mix this through.

Place into a tightly sealed jar and allow to cool. The flavours will improve over the next few days if you can wait that long! The salsa will keep for 1–2 weeks, refrigerated. Serve at room temperature.

I would use this: to spice up sandwiches, sausages and burgers; with nachos or tacos, or in burritos.

Cochinita Pibil

This dish is great cooked over an open fire or even in a fire pit, but this version does not require you to dig big holes in your garden unless an uncontrollable urge overcomes you. It is also a fantastic way of making pulled pork. Once cooked, the meat can be easily shredded with a couple of forks. Ladle the cooking juices over the meat and serve with tortillas or coleslaw or barbecue sauce of your choice!

Yucatecan Achiote Paste
(Recado Rojo) (page 19)

120 ml/½ cup sour orange juice,
or 3 tablespoons orange juice
and 5 tablespoons lime juice

2 kg/4½ lbs. pork shoulder,
bone in

a few banana leaves, hard
stems removed (optional)

Red pickles
2 red onions, thinly sliced
1 teaspoon sea salt
150 ml/⅔ cup red wine vinegar

To serve
wheat tortillas
cooked basmati rice
hot salsa

Serves 6

Mix together the Yucatecan Achiote Paste and juice. Blend thoroughly with a stick blender or in a food processor: this will help to remove the last of the slight grittiness that is often a feature of anything made with annatto seeds. Take the pork and pierce repeatedly with a knife, then rub the paste all over it. This may stain your hands a bit, but it is worth it to get the marinade working well. Cover and marinate in the fridge overnight.

The next day, if you are using banana leaves and they feel like they have dried out, soak them in water for about 30 minutes. Take a suitably large and deep roasting pan. Now lay the banana leaves in the pan so that they overlap each other and overhang the sides of the pan (you will want to fold them over the meat). Put the pork on the banana leaves and fold the leaves over the top to encase the pork. Lay more leaves horizontally across it and tuck them inside the end of the pan to securely encase the pork. (If you are not using banana leaves, wrap the pork in foil instead.)

Preheat the oven to 90–100°C (225°F) Gas ½. Roast the pork for at least 6 hours. When the meat is cooked it will come away from the bone very easily. We have often cooked this for up to 10 hours and it just gets better. If you are worried about the joint drying out, wrap the top of the pan, over the banana leaves, in foil to help seal in the moisture.

To make the red pickles, put the onions in a large glass or plastic bowl and cover with boiling water. Leave for 15 seconds, then drain in a sieve/ strainer. Shake off as much excess moisture as you can. Put the sieve/ strainer back over the bowl, sprinkle the onions with the salt and mix well. Leave for 15 minutes to allow the moisture to drip out of the onions.

Give the onions a little squeeze to remove any excess liquid, then pack them quite tightly in a clean jar. Put the vinegar in a saucepan, bring to the boil and boil vigorously for 2–3 minutes. Pour enough hot vinegar into the jar to cover the onions. Seal the lid tightly and put somewhere cool. Once it has reached room temperature, shake it and put it in the fridge until the cochinita is cooked and ready to serve.

To serve, lift the pickles from the vinegar with a fork and allow to drain. Place in a serving dish. Spoon the excess fat off the pork juices in the roasting pan. Shred the pork, ladle the cooking juices over it and serve with the pickles, wheat tortillas, rice and hot salsa.

Roast Tomato and Chipotle Hot Sauce

This is another absolute classic from Mexico with loads of variations, but I like the way this one balances the smokiness of the Chipotle chillies with the sweetness of the onion and roasted tomatoes. It's one of the best additions to a chicken or sausage sandwich ever invented.

5–6 Chipotle chillies

400 g/14 oz. vine-ripened tomatoes (the riper the better), halved

2 fresh bay leaves

2 thyme sprigs

2 tablespoons olive oil

1 large onion, roughly chopped

3–4 garlic cloves, roughly chopped

1 small glass of red wine

2 tablespoons agave syrup

1 teaspoon mustard powder

1 teaspoon dried oregano

sea salt and freshly ground black pepper

Put the chillies in a bowl and add a little warm water. Allow to soak for 20–30 minutes.

Preheat the oven to 190°C (375°F) Gas 5.

Put the tomatoes and in a roasting pan with the bay leaves and thyme. Drizzle with most of the oil and sprinkle with a little salt. Roast in the preheated oven until the tomatoes are starting to brown – 45–50 minutes. Remove from the oven and allow to cool a little.

Heat the remaining oil in a small frying pan. Fry the onion gently until it begins to turn golden, add the garlic and fry for a further 3–4 minutes. Add the wine and allow to cook for a further few minutes to steam off the alcohol. Remove from the heat.

Take the chillies from the water, remove their stems and deseed them. Put in a food processor or blender with the onion, garlic and wine mixture. Remove the skins from the roasted tomatoes and add the flesh to the food processor. Blend to a smooth paste.

Transfer the paste to a small saucepan with the agave syrup, mustard and oregano and mix thoroughly. Heat over medium heat to a gentle simmer, stirring regularly. Reduce the heat and allow to cook for a further 10 minutes until the sauce reduces to your desired consistency. Taste and season with salt and pepper as required.

The sauce will happily keep for several weeks in an airtight container in the fridge.

I would use this: with a full English (cooked) breakfast!

Yucatecan Achiote Paste (Recado Rojo)

Mexico is a huge country; one of the largest in the world. It is made up of 31 very individual states and as a result there is a depth and variety in the national cuisine that we are only just beginning to recognize. A great example of this diversity is the food of Yucatán. Although perhaps the most visited area of the country by tourists, its food is unlike that of other parts of Mexico. It is the traditional home to the Mayan people, and their influence (along with that of Spanish and Caribbean cuisine) is very apparent in local dishes. This paste features heavily in many dishes including Cochinita Pibil (see page 16).

2 tablespoons annatto seeds

1 tablespoon black peppercorns

5–6 allspice berries

2 teaspoons cumin seeds

2 teaspoons Mexican wild oregano

2 teaspoons sea salt

1 teaspoon ground cinnamon

8 garlic cloves, crushed

½ teaspoon finely chopped Habanero chilli

60 ml/¼ cup sour orange juice, or 1 tablespoon orange juice and 3 tablespoons lime juice

Put the annatto, peppercorns, allspice, cumin, oregano and salt in a heavy-duty mortar and grind together with a pestle. Annatto seeds are very hard, so the heavier the grinding implement the easier it will be. You can always use a coffee or spice grinder. When you have achieved a fairly fine grind, add the cinnamon, garlic and chilli and continue grinding. Add the orange juice and pound to a smooth paste. Cover and refrigerate until ready to use. The paste will keep for several months in an airtight container in the fridge.

I would use this: with pork, turkey, rice and fish.

See also page 16.

Mole Poblano

Mole Poblano has reached a status so legendary that it is easy to be afraid even to attempt making one! It is yet another – I'm sorry – recipe that has no shortcuts and requires a degree of devotion to complete, but it is worth it. Delicious and immensely satisfying, once you have made it from scratch, you will not only feel very smug but you will also see just how poor storebought "moles" can be. Mole Poblano is perhaps the best way of using up leftover turkey and, as such, it deserves to become something of a Boxing Day or Thanksgiving tradition, rather than serving dry sandwiches and ill-considered casseroles.

- 4 Guajillo chillies, deseeded and roughly torn
- 6 Ancho chillies, deseeded and roughly torn
- 3 Pasilla chillies, deseeded and roughly torn
- 3-cm/1¼-inch piece cinnamon stick, roughly broken
- ½ piece star anise
- ¼ teaspoon coriander seeds
- 3 cloves
- 1 teaspoon sesame seeds
- 8 black peppercorns
- ¼ teaspoon dried marjoram
- ½ teaspoon Mexican wild oregano
- a large pinch of dried thyme
- ½ onion, quartered
- 10 garlic cloves, skin on
- 200 g/7 oz. tomatillos
- 120 g/4½ oz. ripe tomatoes
- 1 tablespoon vegetable oil
- 50 g/⅓ cup almonds
- 30 g/1 oz. walnuts
- 20 g/¾ oz. peanuts
- 2 tablespoons pumpkin seeds
- ½ small corn tortilla, torn into small pieces
- 50 g/⅓ cup raisins
- 500 ml/2 cups chicken stock, warmed
- 50 g/2 oz. Mexican chocolate, broken into pieces
- sea salt and ground white pepper

Put the chillies in a heavy-based frying pan and dry-roast them until they begin to char slightly. Remove from the heat immediately. Put the chillies in a bowl, add a little hot water and allow to soak for 20–30 minutes. Drain and reserve the soaking liquid.

In the same pan, toast the cinnamon, star anise, coriander, cloves, sesame seeds and peppercorns over medium heat until they begin to brown and release their aromas. Pour into a bowl and allow to cool. Grind in a coffee or spice grinder until fine. Mix with the herbs and set aside.

Preheat a grill/broiler. Put the onion, garlic, tomatillos and tomatoes in a roasting pan under the hot grill/broiler and toast, turning frequently, until each ingredient is beginning to lightly char. You may want to do this in batches of like ingredients. Allow to cool, then peel the garlic.

In the same heavy-based pan, heat the oil over medium heat and fry the nuts, pumpkin seeds and tortilla pieces until they are well coloured but not burnt. Warning: pumpkin seeds pop as they are fried, so cover the pan with a mesh lid, if you like. Remove from the heat and lift out the nuts, seeds and tortilla pieces from the oil using a slotted spoon. Set the pan and the oil aside.

Put the nuts, seeds, tortilla pieces, raisins and charred onion, garlic, tomatillos and tomatoes in a food processor. Blend until you have a smooth paste, adding the stock as required during blending. Remove the stems from the soaked chillies and add the flesh to the food processor. Blend until they are completely broken down into the paste. Add the ground, roasted spices and blend again. Add some of the chilli soaking liquid and/or stock, if required, as you blend.

Return the reserved pan with its oil to the heat and gently reheat. Force the paste through a fine sieve/strainer into the pan with the back of a spoon to remove any remaining gritty bits. Bring it to a very gentle simmer and simmer over very low heat (and I mean really low!), adding stock as required, for about 60–75 minutes. Stir very regularly. You can cover it, but I tend to leave it uncovered and add stock as required.

Season with salt and add the chocolate. Cook for 10–15 minutes, stirring to ensure the chocolate has melted completely. Add more salt and some white pepper to taste.

I would use this: with lightly poached chicken or turkey served with basmati rice, or in a tortilla (as a taco) sprinkled with toasted sesame seeds.

Ají Amarillo Sauce

The ubiquitous Peruvian chilli sauce, Ají Amarillo is eaten with everything but is particularly good with rice, seafood and potatoes. This can be made with Jalapeño chillies, but there is nothing quite like the real thing made with the famous yellow chillies of Peru. I like the addition of a clove of roasted garlic, accentuating the initial sweet flavours of the sauce; however, this is my own addition and I won't be offended if you want to be truly authentic and leave it out!

250 g/9 oz. Ají Amarillo chillies (or Jalapeños), halved and deseeded

1 roasted garlic clove

2 teaspoons sugar

2 teaspoons lime juice

1 teaspoon cider vinegar

2 tablespoons olive oil

sea salt

Put the chillies and a little water in a saucepan, bring to a gentle simmer and cook for 10 minutes. Add the garlic, sugar, lime juice and vinegar and continue to simmer, stirring regularly to dissolve the sugar. Add a good pinch of salt. Blend to a smooth paste with a stick blender or in a food processor. Gradually add the oil while blending, until the desired consistency is reached. Add more salt if required, and allow to cool.

The sauce will keep for several weeks in an airtight container in the fridge.

I would use this: with anything – but it is particularly good with seafood or potato dishes.

Dan's Favourite Chimichurri

Sometimes referred to as an "Argentine parsley sauce", chimichurri has only recently started to become well known in the northern hemisphere. It does contain parsley and large quantities of it too, but that is where the similarities with the classic English parsley fish sauce ends. Chimichurri is a deliciously herby, garlicky concoction that works equally well as an accompanying sauce or as a marinade. It is traditionally served with beef, although the flavours work brilliantly with chicken and even fish. It rarely features much chilli but the addition of a single Jalapeño gives a lovely hint of warmth, particularly when used as an accompaniment. You can also add a teaspoonful of dried chilli flakes to the blend for a little more heat.

1 small shallot, very finely chopped

1 green Jalapeño chilli, deseeded and finely chopped

juice of 1 small lime

a large handful of flat leaf parsley, finely chopped

3 tablespoons sherry vinegar or red wine vinegar

4 large garlic cloves, crushed

2 teaspoons dried oregano or 2 tablespoons fresh oregano

1 fresh bay leaf, finely chopped and woody stem removed

1 teaspoon red and green peppercorns, freshly ground

125 ml/½ cup extra virgin olive oil

½ teaspoon sea salt

Put the shallot, chilli and lime juice in a small bowl and mix well. Cover and set aside for about 1 hour.

Combine the remaining ingredients in a separate bowl and stir together. Add the shallot mixture and mix thoroughly. This sauce can also be made equally well by giving the ingredients a couple of pulses in a food processor. Cover and allow the flavours to mingle until required.

The acidic nature of this blend allows it to store well for several weeks in an airtight container in the fridge.

I would use this: as a marinade for strips of beef or chicken, or with lamb or fish fillets. See also page 26.

Bolivian Llajua Hot Sauce

This sauce is made using Rocoto peppers, or Locoto as they are known in Bolivia. They are odd chilli plants from the species "Capsicum Pubescens", and their leaves and stems are covered in tiny hairs. Unusually, they are able to withstand cooler temperatures than other species producing a similar heat. Rocoto grow well at altitude and I have grown plants of over 2 metres high with plenty of fruit established in a polytunnel on a blustery hillside 600 ft. above sea level in the north of England. They won't survive a proper frost, but can still be called "hardy" by chilli standards. We have used a combination of coriander/cilantro and basil in this sauce to replicate the flavour of quilquiña – Bolivian coriander.

3–4 large vine-ripened tomatoes, halved and deseeded

1 red Rocoto chilli (or red Habanero), deseeded

2 plump garlic cloves, roughly chopped

a small handful of coriander/cilantro

about 10 basil leaves

olive oil, as required

½ teaspoon sea salt, or to taste

Put all the ingredients except the oil and salt into a food processor/blender and pulse until you have a coarse paste. Add oil to aid blending and to achieve the required consistency. Taste and season with salt.

I would use this: as a fresh salsa for barbecued pork or chicken, or with grilled/broiled chicken.

Pebre

Perhaps the most commonly served sauce in Chile, Pebre is served with most cooked meats and varies greatly in its constituent parts. The recipe below is a good starting point, but feel free to experiment. Make it a few hours in advance, as the flavours improve as they mingle.

2 tablespoons olive oil

1 tablespoon red wine vinegar

100 ml/scant ½ cup water

4–5 fresh Ají chillies (Ají Limo work brilliantly), finely chopped

2 garlic cloves

1 small onion, finely chopped

a large handful of coriander/cilantro, finely chopped

1 tablespoon oregano, finely chopped

½ teaspoon salt

In a medium bowl, beat the oil, vinegar and water together. Add the remaining ingredients and mix thoroughly together. It can be kept for a few days in an airtight container in the fridge.

I would use this: with barbecued meats.

Ají de Huacatay

Here is a very simple version of a sauce that is common throughout Bolivia and Peru. Regular additions to this recipe would be milk (even condensed milk) and/or cotija cheese – a close relative of feta that is salty and crumbly but made with cow's milk. The addition of the cheese makes this sauce delicious when poured over steamed new potatoes. For this recipe I would use about 50 g/1½ oz. of feta cheese, crumbled and blended with the chillies and herbs, before the oil is added.

1 Rocoto chilli (or Habanero), finely chopped

1 Ají Amarillo chilli (or Jalapeño), finely chopped

a small bunch of huacatay (*Tagetes minuta* – black mint/Amazonian mint), or garden mint leaves

a few quilquiña leaves (*Porophyllum ruderale* – Bolivian coriander), or coriander/cilantro, finely chopped

½ celery stick, roughly chopped

about 100 ml/scant ½ cup sunflower oil

sea salt and freshly ground black pepper

Mix together the chillies, herbs and celery. Add enough oil to produce a slick salsa. Season with salt and pepper to taste.

I would use this: with potato dishes and poached meats.

Chimichurri Beef "al Asado"

For this recipe I would recommend making a double batch of our chimichurri sauce and setting it aside, preferably overnight in an airtight container in the fridge, so that the flavours have a chance to mingle. The great thing about chimichurri is its versatility. In this recipe it is the marinade, as well as a baste and a sauce to serve with the finished dish.

As with most great chimichurri dishes, this is cooked over a real fire – in this case a charcoal barbecue. In Argentina "al asado" (on the barbecue) is the favoured method of cooking smaller pieces of meat. For larger pieces, 10 kg (22 lbs.) and over (and Argentineans like large pieces of meat), they cook "al asador" over large metal crosses that are used to take an entire butterflied carcass. These can be used to cook an entire side of beef or a full lamb or suckling pig. There is no rush with this kind of cooking. Larger pieces will take in excess of 5 hours, leaving plenty of time to enjoy a drink or two.

2 × quantities Dan's Favourite
   Chimichurri (page 23)
2 kg/4½ lbs. well-hung deboned
   beef sirloin, in a flat piece
sea salt and freshly ground
   black pepper

To serve
crusty bread
barbecued asparagus
mixed salad

Serves 8

Transfer one quarter of Dan's Favourite Chimichurri to a bowl. Using a pastry brush, paint the steak liberally on both sides with the sauce from the bowl. Top up the sauce in the bowl if necessary and keep it for basting. Note: the remaining sauce will be used as a dressing for the cooked meat, so it is essential that you don't brush sauce onto the meat and then return the brush, which has now been in contact with raw meat, back to the bowl of sauce.

Wrap the meat in clingfilm/plastic wrap and marinate in the fridge for 2 hours. One hour before cooking, light the barbecue; the charcoal needs to be white hot with no flames visible when the meat is put onto the grill/ broiling rack ready to cook. Position the rack 25–30 cm/10–12 inches from the hot coals 10 minutes before cooking to allow it to heat up fully.

Unwrap the beef and season both sides with salt and pepper, then put fat-side down on the grill/broiling rack. Put a lid over the beef on the rack; if your barbecue has a fully closing lid, ensure that the vents are kept open during cooking. Cook until the beef is well coloured on one side and then turn over, cover and cook for 20 minutes. Baste the meat occasionally with some of the Chimichurri sauce from the separate bowl. Turn the meat over again and cook for a further 20 minutes with the lid closed and the vents open. This should give you a rare to medium beef (dependent on the heat of the barbecue); add about 5 more minutes for a medium. Check that the meat is cooked as you like and set it aside to rest for at least 10 minutes.

Slice thickly on the diagonal, and dress with as few spoonfuls of the untouched Chimichurri sauce. Serve with crusty bread, barbecued asparagus and a well-dressed mixed salad.

Noted Chillies: Fatali Habanero (pictured here, right), Malawian Kambuzi, African Bird's Eye (Peri-Peri – pictured here, left)

Chilli Facts and Fiction: In West Africa, crushed chillies are mixed with fresh lime juice and used as an enema. Unsurprisingly, this is guaranteed to cure constipation.

Chapter Two

Africa

Chillies were introduced to Africa by the Portuguese traders as they colonized West and then East Africa. This was undoubtedly a by-product of the slave trade. With over 600,000 acres in production, Ethiopia is second only to India in area set aside for chilli production.

- Once they arrived on the West African coast, chillies were quickly absorbed into the African diet, which already featured "grains of paradise", a member of the ginger family that imparted a pungent, peppery flavour with hints of citrus to many dishes.

- Chillies are used in all African cuisines, from the Moorish dishes of North Africa through the Portuguese-influenced cookery of Mozambique and Angola to the Cape Malay cooking of South Africa.

- Although not indigenous, there are varieties that we have come to associate with the continent. My favourite chilli, the Fatali, appears to have sprung up as a mutation in Central Africa and is now universally associated with Congo. Africa is also home to the chilli with the best name – the Malawian Kambuzi.

- Bird's Eye chillies are ubiquitous throughout Africa, growing wild and in cultivation. They are commonly known as Peri-Peri, Piri-Piri or Pili-Pili. Their small size and bright red colour make them attractive to birds, which do not sense any burning when they eat them. The seeds pass through their digestive systems and are spread wherever the birds fly.

Astonishingly Aromatic Moroccan Tagine Paste

Slow cooking requires little effort and only a modest nod towards "planning" to get a rich flavour and tenderly cooked food. I do however like to plan a little, and with this paste you can create a base for the most delicious tagine that will allow all the flavours to begin to mingle and develop even before they are added to the pot. The basis for all pastes is to get the aromatics and distinctive flavourings out of the spices and infused into the wet ingredients in advance of cooking.

1 tablespoon sunflower oil

1 onion, roughly chopped

1 sweet/bell red pepper, chopped

5–6 garlic cloves, crushed

1–2 tablespoons My Favourite Jordanian Baharat Blend (page 82)

200 g/1⅔ cups passata (Italian sieved tomatoes)

100 g/⅔ cup chickpeas (drained weight)

50 g/⅓ cup ready-to-eat dried apricots, chopped

50 g/⅓ cup dried dates, chopped

3-cm/1¼-inch piece fresh ginger, peeled and finely chopped

zest and juice of 1 lemon

1 teaspoon tomato purée/paste

1 tablespoon cider vinegar

1 teaspoon sugar

1 teaspoon sea salt, or to taste

Heat the oil in a heavy-based saucepan over medium heat. Add the onion and cook for 2–3 minutes. Add the sweet/bell pepper and garlic and fry for a further 3 minutes. Stir in My Favourite Jordanian Baharat Blend, then add the remaining ingredients and heat to a gentle simmer. Cook, stirring regularly, for 5 minutes.

Remove the pan from the heat and blend well with a stick blender or food processor until it forms a glossy, thick and smooth paste. If you feel it is a little dry, add water 1 teaspoon at a time and return it to the heat to heat through. If the mixture is too loose, return to it to the heat and simmer for a few minutes more to cook off some of the excess moisture.

When you are happy with the consistency, spoon the paste into a sterilized jar and seal tightly. Store in the fridge until needed. The paste will continue to improve over a couple of weeks. It is perfect for flavouring slow-cooked North African and Middle Eastern stews.

The paste should keep for many months in a sealed, sterilized container. Once opened, store in the fridge and use within 4 weeks.

I would use this: to cook with lamb, mushrooms, squash and salmon.

Chermoula

A delicious marinade with a robust yet light flavour, chermoula is popular along the entire coastal region of North West Africa where there is almost an infinite number of variations of this classic recipe. In all its forms chermoula seems to be made to partner oily fish, which has always been the staple food in the fishing villages of the southern Mediterranean. It is the perfect stuffing for sardines or mackerel before they are grilled/broiled or barbecued. My favourite addition to the recipe below is probably the classic Moroccan flavour of preserved lemon – particularly good if you are using this with chicken.

2 teaspoons cider vinegar or white wine vinegar

a few saffron threads

a bunch of coriander/cilantro, finely chopped

a small bunch of flat leaf parsley, finely chopped

4 garlic cloves, crushed

1 red chilli, deseeded and finely chopped

2 tablespoons paprika

1 tablespoon ground cumin

1 teaspoon sea salt

½ teaspoon cayenne pepper

juice of 1 lemon

2–3 tablespoons olive oil

Heat the vinegar in a very small saucepan and add the saffron. Remove from the heat and allow to cool. In a medium bowl mix together the coriander/cilantro, parsley, garlic and chilli. Add the other dry ingredients and combine thoroughly.

Pour in the lemon juice, oil and the vinegar and saffron mixture. Stir very well together, then cover the sauce until you are ready to use it. If you do not intend to use immediately, transfer the mixture to a jar, seal tightly and store in the fridge. This blend is best used fresh.

I would use this: to stuff sardines or mackerel. Delicious with roasted veg. See also page 32.

Chermoula Mackerel, Spinach and Preserved Lemon Salad

I have used mackerel for this recipe, but fresh sardines would be equally good and maybe even more authentic. Nothing is more enjoyable than a day's successful fishing followed by an evening of cooking and eating the spoils. Although this recipe calls for the fish to be roasted in the oven, it would be just as easy to do this over an open fire at the beach. Just wrap each fish in a piece of foil, making sure that none of the juices can leak out, and put directly on a rack over the fire or barbecue. Theo, my middle son, loves this sort of "complete cooking" experience, and I think it is so valuable to his education. He understands where everything he eats comes from, what it goes with and how to cook it. Perhaps most importantly, though, we have FUN!

4 whole mackerel, cleaned

Chermoula (page 31)

a handful of thyme sprigs

1 lemon, sliced

250 g/9 oz. fresh spinach leaves, stems removed, finely chopped.

120 ml/½ cup olive oil, plus extra for greasing

a small handful of coriander/cilantro or flat leaf parsley, chopped

4 garlic cloves, finely chopped

1½ teaspoons paprika

1½ teaspoons ground cumin

¼ teaspoon cayenne pepper

a squeeze of lemon juice

1 preserved lemon, pulp finely chopped, rind cut into fine strips

1 handful of pitted black or green olives

sea salt and freshly ground black pepper

plain or lemon couscous, to serve

Serves 4

Make 3 or 4 diagonal slits along each side of the mackerel. Generously coat the inside of the fish with Chermoula and stuff each with a couple of sprigs of thyme and a few slices of lemon. Using your hands, coat each fish with Chermoula, being sure to work it into the slits you have made. Cover and marinate in the fridge for 1 hour.

Bring a saucepan of water to the boil and put a steamer containing the spinach leaves on top. Cover and steam until the leaves darken and are tender. Remove from the heat and squeeze out any excess liquid from the leaves.

Heat the oil in a heavy-based saucepan over medium heat and add the spinach, herbs, garlic, spices, 1½ teaspoons of salt, lemon juice and preserved lemon pulp. Cook for 8 minutes, stirring regularly, to combine the flavours. Season with pepper. Tip into a bowl and allow to cool slightly. Serve slightly warm or at room temperature, dressed with the olives and preserved lemon rind.

Preheat the oven to 180°C (350°F) Gas 4.

Heat a heavy-based ovenproof frying pan over medium-high heat and coat with a little oil, then add the fish and sear on both sides for 2 minutes per side. Transfer the pan to the oven and bake for a further 10 minutes, or until the mackerel is just cooked through. Remove from the pan and allow the fish to rest for a few minutes. Serve on a bed of plain or lemon couscous with the spinach salad and a drizzle of Chermoula sauce.

La Kama Spice Blend

The cubeb berries used in this recipe are the precursor to the black and white pepper we use today. Also known as Java Pepper, the spice is mentioned as long ago as the 4th century BC and was in regular culinary use until the 16th century when black pepper, which was much cheaper, became widely available. Although this is not strictly chilli, La Kama is a deliciously light and peppery seasoning that originated in Tangier. It can be used on chicken or fish, or even to flavour a pan of lentils or couscous. It's great to sprinkle over veg before roasting. Try combining it with a little lemon zest as a marinade for chicken or adding a little cumin and rolling a lamb joint in it before roasting.

2 teaspoons cubeb berries
1 tablespoon ground ginger
1 tablespoon ground turmeric
1 tablespoon freshly ground
   black pepper
2 teaspoons ground cinnamon
1 teaspoon grated nutmeg

Grind the cubeb berries to a powder using a mortar and pestle, then tip into a bowl. Add the remaining ingredients and mix thoroughly, then transfer to an airtight container. Store in a cool, dark place until you are ready to use it. The cubeb berries lose their intensity quite quickly once ground, so this mixture is best made as and when required.

I would use this: sprinkled over chicken or vegetables to roast, with pulses.

Ras el Hanout Spice Blend

This is a simple version of a legendary spice blend. Meaning "top of the store" in Arabic, or more often "house blend", it can contain anything up to 50–60 ingredients. It has so many uses, but I would definitely recommend trying it in a slow-cooked rabbit casserole, with poached or scrambled eggs and as flavouring when cooking lentils. It is also a key constituent in the Classic North African Rub recipe (page 39).

2 teaspoons ground cumin
2 teaspoons ground turmeric
2 teaspoons ground ginger
2 teaspoons sea salt
2 teaspoons brown sugar
1 teaspoon freshly ground black pepper
1 teaspoon ground cinnamon
1 teaspoon ground coriander
1 teaspoon cayenne pepper
1 teaspoon ground allspice
1 teaspoon ground fennel seeds
1 teaspoon blue poppy seeds
½ teaspoon ground cardamom
½ teaspoon ground cloves
½ teaspoon dried rose petals, ground, or dried culinary lavender flowers

Put all the ingredients in a large bowl and mix thoroughly. Store in a tightly sealed jar in a cool, dark place, until required.

I would use this: in a rabbit casserole, with eggs and pulses or as a delicious coating for vegetables before roasting. See also page 39.

Walnut, Sesame and Chilli Dressing

This recipe was given to me by a friend who seems to spend an immoderate amount of time scribbling in his notebook. Eventually, thinking this was all a bit rude, I demanded to know what he was constantly recording: recipes, and lots of them — from radio, books, magazines, TV, conversations, holidays and menus! Anyway this recipe comes from that notebook and is wonderfully simple. Its flavour seems to effortlessly bridge the divide between Mediterranean and North African styles.

It is one of those sauces that really goes with anything but I think it accompanies a simple preparation best. Try it with a grilled/broiled chicken salad.

1 tablespoon olive oil

75 g/⅔ cup walnut pieces

1 tablespoon tahini

2 tablespoons extra virgin olive oil

juice of ½ lemon

1 small garlic clove, crushed

1 red chilli, deseeded and finely chopped

a small handful of flat leaf parsley or tarragon, finely chopped

a few mint leaves, torn

Heat the olive oil in a small frying pan over medium heat and add the walnuts. Cook gently until they start to change colour, then tip them onto kitchen paper/paper towels to drain and cool. Discard the oil.

In a small bowl, whisk the tahini with the extra virgin olive oil and the lemon juice. Add the cooled walnuts, the garlic, chilli and parsley, and mix together. Loosen with a few tablespoons of water as required. Add the mint leaves and stir them through the mixture. Serve immediately.

I would use this: to accompany grilled/broiled fish or chicken or to dress a strong, peppery salad.

Cardamom-infused Apricot and Almond Chilli Jam

Sweet, spicy and full of North African flavours, this dressing is ideally suited to a strong cheese board but it is also great in a pitta bread or with falafels and natural yogurt. You could even try this in a rice pudding or as a filling for Moroccan-style pastries. I love the cardamom infused through it, but do experiment. Add ½ teaspoon My Favourite Jordanian Baharat Blend (page 82) instead of cardamom, if you like.

500 g/3¾ cups ready-to-eat dried apricots

500 g/2½ cups packed muscovado sugar

75 g/¾ cup almonds, roughly chopped

100 ml/scant ½ cup lemon juice

zest and juice of 1 lime

¼ teaspoon ground cardamom

½ small Habanero chilli, deseeded and finely chopped

1 large red chilli, such as a Guindilla, as long as it is fleshy and not too hot, deseeded and finely chopped

Put the apricots in a bowl and add 600 ml/2½ cups water, then leave overnight to soften and rehydrate. Tip the soaked apricots and their soaking water into a large saucepan and bring to the boil, then gently simmer for 30–40 minutes until they are soft. Stir in the sugar and heat over a low heat to dissolve, stirring constantly to ensure no sugar catches on the base of the pan. Once you are sure that all the sugar has been dissolved, turn the heat up. Add the almonds, lemon juice, lime zest and juice, cardamom and chillies. Boil rapidly over high heat, stirring regularly, to prevent the contents sticking to the base of the pan.

To test if the jam has reached setting point, drip a little onto a saucer and chill briefly in the fridge, or preferably in the freezer. If it forms a skin, it is ready. If not, return to the heat, continue cooking and test again in 10 minutes. Pour into sterilized jars and seal.

I would use this: as a relish to serve with strong cheeses or as a glaze for roasting chicken.

Harissa Paste (opposite)

In many ways Harissa is the taste of North Africa. It is commonly associated with Tunisia, but you can find variations throughout Morocco, Algeria and Libya. These include adding caramelized shallots or fresh rose petals, resulting in the famous rose Harissa. It can add a great little fiery kick to any dish and is an essential addition to lablabi, the Tunisian breakfast soup of chickpeas, garlic and egg.

50 g/1¾ oz. dried chilli flakes, preferably Bakloutis, or even Bird's Eye if you are feeling brave

1 teaspoon cumin seeds

1 teaspoon coriander seeds

1 teaspoon caraway seeds, freshly ground

1 red sweet/bell pepper, roasted, skinned and deseeded

1 teaspoon sea salt

4 plump garlic cloves, chopped

1 teaspoon smoked paprika

1 tablespoon red wine vinegar

2 tablespoons tomato purée/paste

zest and juice from ½ lemon

½ preserved lemon, finely chopped

good-quality olive oil, if needed

Put the chill flakes in a bowl and cover with a little hot water (DO NOT BREATHE IN THE FUMES!). Cover and leave for 15–20 minutes to rehydrate. Meanwhile, put the cumin, coriander and caraway seeds in a dry frying pan and toast over medium heat.

Drain the water from the chilli flakes and put the flakes into a food processor. Add the toasted spices and the remaining ingredients except the oil. Blend until you have a smooth paste. Add a little olive oil to the paste while blending, if required, to achieve a smooth consistency. Tip into a small saucepan and heat gently until just bubbling. Add a little water, if required, to prevent burning, and simmer gently for 10 minutes.

Transfer to a small sterilized jar and top up with olive oil, ensuring the paste is completely covered. Seal tightly and store in the fridge for up to 4 months. It is a good idea to top up the jar with olive oil each time you use some of the paste to make sure it is not exposed to the air. This will greatly help improve the length of time you can store your harissa.

I would use this: as the base for a marinade for fish or chicken.

Classic North African Rub

This robust seasoned rub makes good use of the Ras el Hanout dry spice blend. It is has a deliciously intense flavour, which works particularly well if combined with a little yogurt to make a simple marinade.

2 tablespoons sea salt

3 teaspoons caraway seeds

2 teaspoons dried oregano

1 teaspoon cumin seeds

1 teaspoon dried rosemary

½ teaspoon dried chilli flakes

3 teaspoons Ras el Hanout Spice Blend (page 35)

1 teaspoon ground turmeric

5 garlic cloves, roasted in their skins for 15 minutes, or until soft

3–4 tablespoons olive oil

Grind the salt, caraway, oregano, cumin, rosemary and chilli flakes together to create a fine powder, either using a spice grinder or a mortar and pestle. Tip into a bowl and stir in the Ras el Hanout Spice Blend and turmeric.

Squeeze out the soft roasted garlic flesh into the bowl and add enough olive oil to make a smooth paste. Combine all the ingredients thoroughly. This mixture will keep well if put into a small sterilized jar and topped up with olive oil.

I would use this: on poultry, game or lamb before cooking.

The Ultimate Peri-Peri Marinade

The story of Peri-Peri (or Piri-Piri, or Pili-Pili) in all its forms encapsulates the story of chillies and their spread across the world over the last 400 years. Piri-Piri itself simply means "chilli chilli" in the dialect of southern Mozambique and it generally refers to the African Bird's Eye. It is most likely to have been introduced to these regions by the Portuguese (who are also responsible for introducing chillies to India); they had in turn brought the spice over from the Americas. Today, we refer to Peri-Peri as the marinade or sauce that, although likely to be Portuguese in origin, is most closely associated with its former colonies of Mozambique and Angola.

This is my take on a classic recipe. As with all marinades of this kind it benefits from a little ageing before being pressed into service. I would recommend making this a couple of days before you need it, and storing it in a jar in the fridge, giving it a little shake a couple of times a day!

2 teaspoons nut oil

3 limes, quartered

1 large onion, very finely chopped

10 red Bird's Eye chillies (or 5 Bird's Eye and 2 Fatali), deseeded and finely chopped

1 garlic bulb, cloves crushed

zest of 1 lemon and juice of 2 lemons

a large bunch of flat leaf parsley, finely chopped

2 fresh bay leaves, central stalk discarded, finely chopped

180 ml/scant ¾ cup olive oil

100 ml/scant ½ cup cider vinegar

2 tablespoons sea salt

½ teaspoon smoked paprika

3 tablespoons sweet paprika

1 teaspoon dried oregano

Heat a frying pan over medium heat and add the nut oil. Fry each cut side of the limes until they start to develop a good colour; it can help to gently press the limes onto the pan with the back of a fork, as this releases a little more of the juice and aids the caramelization of the sugars. Remove from the pan and set aside with any juice in the pan.

Put the onion, chillies and garlic in a large bowl and squeeze into this the juice from the caramelized limes. Add the lemon zest and fresh juice. Add the parsley and bay leaves and mix thoroughly.

Pour the olive oil into a separate bowl and add the vinegar, salt, smoked and sweet paprika and oregano. Whisk together to combine.

Add to the chilli mixture and stir thoroughly to combine well. Pour into a glass jar and seal. Put in the fridge and leave to mature for at least 24 hours, but preferably 48 hours, giving the jar a regular shake. Use within 4–5 days.

I would use this: as a marinade for chicken, beef or prawns/shrimp or as a dip for these and for spicy sausages.

Ethiopian Berbere Paste

I started seriously experimenting with chillies in my cooking after returning from west and southern Africa. I loved Africa, and the idea of entire cuisines that no one at the time seemed to know anything about was an opportunity that I found impossible to resist. Using my first crop of home-grown chillies I made, among other things, a fresh Ethiopian Berbere Paste. It was fantastically flavoursome and quite the most eye-wateringly hot little pot of chilli one could imagine placing on any dinner table. It is used both in cooking (a requirement for Dabo Kolo – a traditional crunchy bread snack) and as an accompaniment for almost any meat, vegetable or rice dish. Berbere may sound exotic, but it simply means "hot" in the Amharic language of Ethiopia.

1 teaspoon cardamom pods

5–6 cloves

½ teaspoon coriander seeds

½ teaspoon cumin seeds

1½ teaspoons fenugreek seeds

2 tablespoons dried chilli flakes

2 tablespoons paprika

1 tablespoon sea salt

½ teaspoon black peppercorns, coarsely ground

½ teaspoon ground turmeric

¼ teaspoon ground allspice

a good grating of nutmeg

a good pinch of ground cinnamon

1 large onion, finely chopped

5-cm/2-inch piece fresh ginger, peeled and finely chopped

4 garlic cloves, crushed

2 tablespoons deseeded and finely chopped Habanero chillies

about 4 tablespoons groundnut oil

Put the cardamom pods in a small saucepan and add the cloves, coriander, cumin and fenugreek. Toast over medium heat, keeping the spices moving to avoid charring them. Remove from the heat.

When cool enough to handle, take the cardamom seeds out of the pods and put these into a food processor or mortar with the other toasted spices. Add the other dry ingredients and pulse repeatedly, or grind with a pestle, to create a fairly coarse but even powder – or to your preferred consistency.

Add the onion, ginger, garlic and fresh chillies, and blend or grind again. Add the oil while blending to alter the consistency. The final Berbere should be smooth, thick and glossy without being sticky.

I would use this: added to any type of stew or as a REALLY spicy table dip.

Niter Kibbeh

This spiced clarified butter is a great addition to any storecupboard, as it keeps for longer then conventional butter and can be used to cook at higher temperatures without burning. It is similar to the ghee used in Indian cooking, but the addition of the spices makes it far more flavoursome. It is a staple of Ethiopian cuisine and provides a simple way of flavouring many dishes. It is particularly useful in savoury baking.

¼ teaspoon fenugreek seeds

1–2-cm/½–¾-inch piece cinnamon stick, roughly broken up

1–2 cloves

1 small hot dried chilli, deseeded

¼ teaspoon cardamom seeds

½ teaspoon ground turmeric

a generous pinch of grated nutmeg

250 g/2 sticks unsalted butter, cut into chunks

1 shallot (or small onion), very finely chopped

2 garlic cloves, very finely chopped

2.5-cm/1-inch piece fresh ginger, peeled and finely grated

Put the fenugreek in a heavy-based saucepan with the cinnamon, cloves, chilli and cardamom seeds. Toast until they begin to release their aroma. Remove from the pan and grind to a fine powder in a spice grinder or using a mortar and pestle. Stir in the turmeric and nutmeg.

Melt the pieces of butter in the pan over gentle heat, stirring regularly to ensure they don't catch on the pan. Turn the heat up and bring the butter to a boil. Add the shallot, garlic and ginger, and fry for 2 minutes, then stir in the ground spice mixture. Make sure everything is evenly mixed, because the mixture must not be stirred again during cooking. Reduce the heat and cook at a very gentle simmer for 50 minutes.

A clear "butter" should float to the surface. Strain this liquid through a muslin into a second pan to remove all the butter solids and spices. Repeat if necessary to obtain a completely clear liquid. Pour into a sterilized jar, seal and store in the fridge. The liquid will turn solid as it chills and will keep for several months in the fridge.

I would use this: to make fantastically flavoursome cheese scones, in scrambled eggs or in the place of ghee in Indian curries.

Classic South African Braii Sauce

Braii is the Afrikaans word for "barbecue" and is perhaps the defining cooking method in South African food. Braiis are universally wood-fired and are literally everywhere. On my first trip to South Africa I remember going to watch India play in a one-day international cricket match in Paarl. Two things are indelibly printed on my mind from that day (apart from the cricket). The first was that I had never seen so many homemade real fire barbecues in one place – when they were lit you simply couldn't see the other side of the ground! The second was the sheer volume of beer consumed while cooking on them. It is a method and approach to barbecuing I have taken to heart and recommend to everyone!

This is a fantastic recipe (from Paarl) for a sauce to be used as a marinade or table sauce; however, it really comes into its own as a fabulous baste for meat while it is being barbecued. The chillies are added to taste and there can be anything from none up to a good handful!

1 large onion, roughly chopped

4 garlic cloves, roughly chopped

1 red sweet/bell pepper, deseeded and chopped

2–3 Bird's Eye chillies, deseeded and chopped

3 tablespoons red wine vinegar

about 1 tablespoon olive oil

400-g/14-oz. can plum tomatoes, drained

1 tablespoon tomato purée/paste

2 tablespoons Worcestershire sauce

2 tablespoons homemade fruity chutney

1 teaspoon cayenne pepper

3–4 tablespoons muscovado/molasses sugar

1 teaspoon mustard powder

Put all the ingredients into a blender or food processor and pulse until you have a smooth, glossy paste. Loosen with a little more oil or water if required. Store in an airtight jar in the fridge until you are ready to use. This recipe benefits from being made a little in advance – a day or two is ideal!

I would use this: with all meats, or even spicy sausage. It makes an excellent marinade for game birds too – try this with pheasant breast.

Pinang Kerrie Sauce

The Cape Malay cooking of southern South Africa results in some of the best spicy food in the world. This recipe shows a simple blending of styles and creates the perfect flavouring for a "hot" lamb curry: marinate the lamb in the paste, fry some onions, add the lamb for a few minutes, then add 400 ml/ 1³/₄ cups chicken stock and simmer until the sauce is very thick and the meat is cooked through.

1 tablespoon Malay Curry
  Powder (page 135)

1 teaspoon ground turmeric

1 teaspoon sea salt

1 teaspoon palm sugar

2 tablespoons cider vinegar

1 teaspoon tamarind paste

1 tablespoon dark soy sauce

2.5-cm/1-inch piece fresh
  ginger, peeled and grated

4–5 garlic cloves, crushed

3 Zimbabwe Bird (or Bird's Eye)
  chillies

1 tablespoon sunflower oil

2 bay leaves

2 tablespoons coriander/
  cilantro stalks and leaves,
  chopped

Put all the ingredients in a blender or food processor and pulse until you have a smooth, thick paste. Add a little water if the consistency is too thick. Store in an airtight container until ready to use. The flavours will improve if made a couple of days in advance.

I would use this: to cook with lamb, pork and chicken.

Tsire Powder

A wonderfully simple West African spice blend, Tsire Powder is ideal for adding a delicious seasoning and a tasty bit of crunch to meat kebabs/kabobs. It is also excellent when sprinkled over roasting vegetables or even salads. If you like, make a larger batch — it stores well.

100 g/3½ oz. salted roasted peanuts

2 teaspoons chilli powder

½ teaspoon grated nutmeg

½ teaspoon ground ginger

½ teaspoon ground cinnamon

¼ teaspoon ground cloves

¼ teaspoon ground allspice

Grind the peanuts into a coarse powder using a grinder or a mortar and pestle. Tip into a bowl and stir in the other ingredients, ensuring everything is evenly blended. Pour into an airtight container, seal and store in a cool, dark place until required.

I would use this: to coat chicken before frying, or add a spoonful or two to a homemade burger mix for extra flavour and texture. See also below.

West African Lamb Koftas

Koftas (in their kebab/kabob form) originated in the Middle East and there are reckoned to be in excess of 290 recipes used in Turkey alone. This recipe combines the West African love of chilli with the delicious traditional coating of Tsire Powder, giving the koftas a wonderful seasoning and crunch.

600 g/1 lb. 5 oz. lamb, diced

1 small onion, finely chopped

1 garlic clove, crushed

1 small hot chilli, deseeded and finely chopped

2 tablespoons full-fat natural yogurt

Tsire Powder (see above)

1 egg, beaten

olive oil

1 rosemary sprig

sea salt and freshly ground black pepper

To serve
pitta bread
mixed salad
yogurt dip

10–12 wooden skewers

Makes 10–12

Soak the skewers in water for 30 minutes to prevent them from burning. Light a barbecue; you will need to give it about 45 minutes for the charcoal or wood to have burnt down sufficiently to cook over, ideally leaving hot, white embers.

Put the lamb into a food processor with the onion, garlic, chilli, yogurt and a good pinch of salt and pepper. Process until the mixture is smooth and evenly mixed.

Divide the lamb mixture into 10–12 portions and roll each into a thick sausage shape. (It is often easier to do this with cold, wet hands.) Take a skewer and either slide it lengthways through a lamb "sausage" or press the meat around the skewer. Repeat this for the other portions.

Tip a few tablespoons of the Tsire Powder onto a tray. Dip, or brush, each kofta in the beaten egg to thoroughly coat. Roll them in the Tsire Powder until they are evenly coated. Drizzle lightly with a little olive oil.

Throw the rosemary sprig onto the hot charcoal just before you put the koftas onto the grill/broiling rack. Cook, turning regularly, for 10–15 minutes until the meat is cooked through.

Serve immediately with pitta bread, a peppery mixed salad and maybe a yogurt dip. Sprinkle with a little more Tsire Powder if you like.

Egusi Sauce (opposite: left)

Egusi is commonly found in West Africa as a soup, but in Central and East Africa it is far more commonly used as a sauce. It is traditionally thickened using flour made from the seeds of the squash family. Pumpkin seeds are readily available and are great for making this delicious, high-protein sauce for grilled/broiled meats, rice or vegetables. To prepare the pumpkin seeds for this recipe, roast them on a baking tray at 180°C (350°F) Gas 4 until they begin to colour; you may need to turn them to aid even cooking. Allow them to cool and then blitz to a fine powder in a food processor.

2 tablespoons vegetable oil

1 large onion, finely chopped

2 large tomatoes, chopped

1 red sweet/bell pepper, finely chopped

1 Fatali Habanero chilli, (or any Habanero or hot chilli), stalk removed

225 g/1¾ cups pumpkin seed flour (or egusi)

sea salt and freshly ground black pepper

Heat the oil in a saucepan over medium heat and fry the onion for 5 minutes. Add the tomatoes, sweet/bell pepper and chilli. Mix together, then cover and cook for 10 minutes, stirring occasionally.

Stir in the flour and mix thoroughly. Add water as required to create a smooth sauce; you can use a stick blender to pulse the sauce to get an even and smooth consistency, if you like. bring to a gentle simmer. Cook for 3–5 minutes until thickened. Season with salt and pepper, and serve.

I would use this: to accompany rice and grilled/broiled meats.

Pili-Pili Sauce (opposite: right)

Ubiquitous throughout tropical Africa, Pili-Pili can be found in one form or another. This recipe comes from East Africa and was one of the first recipes I tried when I first began making chilli sauces. It eventually evolved into the all-purpose African Hot Sauce that we now make. This purist version has no onion and no tomatoes or sweet peppers — just a lot of chillies, lemon and garlic. Used as a dipping sauce throughout the region it is certainly not for the faint-hearted.

100 g/3½ oz. Fatali Habanero chillies (or other hot chillies), stalks removed

3 garlic cloves, roughly chopped

juice of 1 lemon

a small handful of roughly chopped mixed herbs (such as parsley, coriander/cilantro and oregano)

2 tablespoons vegetable oil

sea salt

Put all the ingredients in a food processor and pulse until you have a coarse but well mixed sauce. Add a little water to aid mixing, if required. (To make using a mortar and pestle, first grind the chillies and garlic with some salt, then add the herbs, lemon juice and oil.)

Cook the blended mixture in a frying pan over medium-high heat for 2 minutes, or until the garlic is softened, then pour into a sterilized container to cool. Seal until airtight. This will store well in the fridge for weeks and probably months!

I would use this: with anything that needs a touch of fire!

Noted Chillies: Scotch Bonnets (pictured here), Caribbean Red Habanero, Trinidad Moruga Scorpion, Wiri Wiri, Bird peppers

Chilli Facts and Fiction: In Trinidad, chilli pepper leaf tea is served as a remedy for coughs and sore throats.

As a cure for baldness, hot chilli oil is applied topically to the head. The resulting tingling, burning sensation is supposed to stimulate hair growth.

Caribbean

The spiritual home of all things hot, the Caribbean was one of the first areas to be reached by the natural spread of chillies – "natural" meaning unaided by humankind.

- The definitive flavour of Caribbean cooking is the Scotch Bonnet chilli or other closely related Habanero varieties: in Jamaica, Scotch Bonnet or Bonnie pepper; in Trinidad, Congo peppers; in Barbados, Bonney peppers; and in the French Antilles my favourite Scotch Bonnet, the Antillais Caribbean.

- All these chilli peppers are intensely hot and have an amazingly fruity aroma and flavour. They are an integral ingredient in most indigenous Caribbean dishes.

- These fresh chillies are also used to make the famous hot pepper sauces of the area that ensure this indispensable flavour and fiery kick is available even if fresh peppers are not.

- The use of so many hot peppers in traditional Caribbean cuisine is often explained as a natural response to the tropical climate of the region: eating food packed with chillies causes the body to sweat and so aids its own cooling.

- Among the other chillies used in Caribbean cuisine are the Wiri Wiri, a *Capsicum Frutescens* species that, although milder than a Scotch Bonnet, still packs a punch. Wiri Wiri are particularly popular in Guyanese cuisine.

- Throughout the world, hot peppers are also considered to be a powerful aphrodisiac – the hotter the chilli the more potent its effects. Perhaps this too explains the Caribbean love of the fiery Scotch Bonnets!

Mother-in-Law Sauce

There can be few condiments or sauces named in a less exotic or more provocative manner than this piece of sheer genius from Trinidad. It is a kind of salsa—ridiculously hot salad combination, although it can be blended down to make a genuine pourable sauce, which I suspect would store for longer. However, we have never had any left to store, so it is a moot point. The name comes from this recipe's fiery tongue that is guaranteed to leave an impression on you. Good or bad? I couldn't possibly make a personal comment – far too scared.

1 large carrot

1 onion

½–1 small green karali/bitter melon (or unripe, green mango), deseeded

4 Trinidad Congo (or Scotch Bonnet) hot chillies, deseeded

4 garlic cloves

8 chadon beni leaves (or a small handful of coriander/cilantro)

juice of 2 limes

1 teaspoon sea salt

cider vinegar, as needed (optional)

The key to making this dish work well is to make sure that the ingredients are chopped to approximately the same size. Peel and chop the carrot and onion and put in a large bowl. Chop the karali and add to the mixture. The chillies will need to be chopped slightly more finely, and it is advisable to wear gloves to do this as they are extremely hot! Add these to the bowl and then chop the garlic to approximately the same size as the chillies. Mix thoroughly in the bowl.

Finely chop the chadon beni leaves and add to the bowl with the lime juice and salt. Mix thoroughly and put in the fridge for a few hours before serving, stirring occasionally.

If you wish to blend this down to a sauce, I would suggest adding a small amount of cider vinegar to loosen the mixture as it is blended. This will also lower its natural pH level giving it a slightly increased storage life in the fridge.

As a salsa, I would recommend using this on the day it is made.

I would use this: as an accompaniment to any barbecued meat or fish, or even as a fiery burger relish.

Dan's Caribbean Classic

Sometimes all you want is a simple, perfect chilli sauce – and this sauce is just that. Based on a classic Trinidadian recipe, it calls for Scotch Bonnet chillies, which are essential, but if possible, use Antillais Caribbean strain for their mouthwatering aroma, fruitiness, and balance of flavour, heat and acidity.

1 tablespoon cider vinegar

½ teaspoon mustard seeds

50 g/1¾ oz. Scotch Bonnet chillies (stalks removed), halved

1 teaspoon lemon juice

1 garlic clove, crushed

½ teaspoon salt

1 teaspoon lime juice

Gently warm the vinegar in a small saucepan over medium heat and add the mustard seeds. Cover and set aside for at least 1 hour to allow the seeds to soften a little. Add the chillies, 1 tablespoon water, the lemon juice, garlic and salt to the pan, and return to the heat. Heat to a gentle simmer and cook until the chillies have softened a little. Use a stick blender (or transfer to a blender) to process the ingredients to a smooth sauce consistency. (You may need to do this in a smaller container to allow the blender blades to be covered and to operate effectively.)

Return to the heat and add the lime juice. Bring back to a gentle simmer and cook for 2 minutes, stirring regularly. If the sauce seems a little thick, add a few tablespoons more water. Blend again if required. Pour into a sterilized bottle and seal tightly. Allow to cool, then store in the fridge until you are ready to use it. The flavours will mingle and improve over the next few weeks. I have kept an open bottle of this sauce in my fridge for several months with no noticeable change in appearance or taste, so you can double or treble these ingredients and make up a larger batch.

I would use this: with anything and everything that needs a little hit.

Rum, Lime and Ginger Marinade

Mango, chilli, rum, coconut milk and lime – sounds simple but tastes exotic and fiery. Quite possibly these ingredients make the perfect cocktail as well as the basis for a Caribbean marinade!

½ mango, peeled, pitted and chopped

1 tablespoon dark rum

1 Scotch Bonnet chilli, deseeded

2 garlic cloves, crushed

2.5-cm/1-inch piece fresh ginger, peeled and chopped

½ teaspoon ground coriander

a pinch of ground cumin

a pinch of sea salt

50 ml/scant ¼ cup coconut milk

juice of 1 lime

a small bunch of coriander/cilantro, finely chopped

Put the mango, rum, chilli, garlic and ginger in a small food processor and blend to a smooth paste.

Transfer to a small pan and heat gently over medium heat, then add the remaining spices, salt and coconut milk. Bring to a gentle simmer and add the lime juice. Cook for 5 minutes and add the coriander/cilantro. Remove from the heat, pour into a sterilized container and seal tightly. Allow to cool before using.

I would use this: as a marinade for vegetables or fish.

Simple Orange and Cumin Marinade (opposite)

Simple and tasty, this marinade from Cuba needs to be made with Seville or sour oranges because it is their sharpness that makes the marinade. If you can't get hold of any (it can be difficult out of season), use a combination of half orange juice and half lime juice.

zest of 1 orange

juice of 4–5 Seville (or sour) oranges

1 onion, finely chopped

8 garlic cloves, finely chopped

2 teaspoons ground cumin

2 teaspoons chilli powder

1 teaspoon sea salt

½ teaspoon freshly ground black pepper

Put all the ingredients in a food processor and blend until you have a smooth but quite loose sauce. Store in a airtight jar in the fridge until you are ready to use it.

I would use this: as a marinade for pork, especially shoulder, before roasting.

Seriously Hot Chilli and Citrus Marinade

Every couple of days in our house, we get the uncontrollable urge to eat something really fiery, and to be honest this is about as hot as it gets. It can be used as a simple marinade or, if you fancy something a little more adventurous, you can cut a slit along the side of a chicken breast and stuff it with the marinade and rub a little more over the outside, then wrap it in pancetta and roast it in the oven.

4 Scotch Bonnet chillies, deseeded and cut into fine strips

2 banana shallots, finely sliced

2-cm/¾-inch piece fresh ginger, peeled and cut into fine strips

5–6 garlic cloves, crushed

1 teaspoon salt

zest and juice of 2 lemons

2 tablespoons muscovado/ molasses sugar

2 tablespoons cider vinegar

1 teaspoon thyme leaves

1 teaspoon red peppercorns, ground

½ teaspoon ground allspice

Put the chillies, shallots, ginger and garlic in a bowl. Sprinkle with the salt and squeeze over the lemon juice. Stir the mixture thoroughly, then set aside for 15 minutes. Add the sugar to the vinegar and stir to break it up. Add the sugar mixture to the chilli mixture followed by the remaining ingredients, and stir together thoroughly. Cover and refrigerate for 1–2 hours to allow the flavours to mingle.

I would use this: as a brilliant marinade for pork or firm white fish. The sugars in the marinade caramelize deliciously if cooked under a hot grill/broiler or on the barbecue. But beware: this is frighteningly HOT, so use with caution.

Antillais Caper and Scotch Bonnet Sauce

Try this as an accompaniment to any fresh grilled/broiled fish — mackerel would be perfect. I still can't imagine a better place in the world to eat fresh fish than the Caribbean: straight off the boat and onto glowing embers! This sauce takes the classic flavour of capers and gives it a huge kick of fiery, fruity Scotch Bonnet — perfect with the lime juice and fresh herbs.

1 banana shallot (or other large shallot), roughly chopped

1 garlic clove, roughly chopped

a small handful of coriander/cilantro, chopped

a few flat leaf parsley and/or tarragon leaves, chopped

juice of 1½–2 limes

2 tablespoons good-quality olive oil

1 tablespoon capers, rinsed and chopped

1 tablespoon Cabernet Sauvignon vinegar

1–2 Antillais Caribbean Scotch Bonnet chillies, deseeded

sea salt and freshly ground black pepper

Put all the ingredients in a blender or food processor and pulse until you have a smooth and fragrant sauce. Add 1–2 tablespoons water to loosen the sauce if it is a little thick. Season with salt and pepper, to taste. Set aside for 10–15 minutes to allow the flavours to combine. Enjoy!

I would use this: to serve with fresh grilled/broiled or barbecued fish. See also page 58.

Antillais Fish Marinade

The French Antilles are in many ways the gem of the Caribbean when it comes to cuisine. Heavily influenced by its French colonial history, the food is often complex and always delicious. This is a simple marinade designed for fish – and being Caribbean it is wonderfully HOT! It uses the Antillais Caribbean Scotch Bonnet, which to my mind is simply the best Scotch Bonnet out there – it also grows rather well on a warm windowsill in the UK!

4½ tablespoons lime juice

1 teaspoon sea salt

3 thyme sprigs, leaves stripped and chopped

1 teaspoon mixed peppercorns, ground

3 garlic cloves, chopped

1–2 Antillais Caribbean Scotch Bonnet (or other Scotch Bonnet) chillies, deseeded

Put all the ingredients in a food processor or blender and process until you have a smooth paste. Scrape into a large resealable food bag and refrigerate until you are ready to use it.

To use, add the fish to the bag, reseal it and give the bag a really good shake. Marinate for about 20 minutes.

I would use this: to coat red snapper, but any firm-fleshed fish would do – try monkfish. See also page 58.

Marinated Monkfish with Grilled Vegetable Salad

Despite the very Caribbean use of hot chilli, the food of the French Antilles often has a distinct feel of southern France. In this recipe the spicy monkfish is accompanied with a simple salad of grilled/broiled vegetables and herbs. This dish is very hot and illustrates how well suited fresh fish and fresh chillies are. If you're worried about scaring your guests (or children), you can slightly reduce the chilli content in the marinade. A little extra dressing can always be used to "reboot" the chilli level when serving.

2 monkfish fillet steaks, about
    150 g/5½ oz. each
Antillais Fish Marinade
    (page 57)
1 aubergine/eggplant
1 red sweet/bell pepper
225 g/8 oz. ripe tomatoes
1 courgette/zucchini
olive oil, for brushing and
    frying
a good handful of finely
    chopped mixed herbs, such
    as basil, parsley, tarragon
Antillais Caper and Scotch
    Bonnet Sauce (page 56)
sea salt and freshly ground
    black pepper

Serves 2

Put the monkfish in a resealable food bag and add the Antillais Fish Marinade. Reseal the bag and give it a good shake. Make sure the fish is well coated in the marinade. Put in the fridge and marinate for 2 hours. (Monkfish is very meaty and can take longer to marinate than most other fish.)

Meanwhile, cut the aubergine/eggplant into slices about 1 cm/½ inch thick, sprinkle with salt and leave in a colander for 1 hour. Rinse well and put on kitchen paper/paper towels to dry. Pat the tops dry.

Put the pepper under a hot grill/broiler until its skin blackens. Remove from the heat, put in a suitable food bag and allow to cool.

Put the tomatoes under the hot grill/broiler and cook until the skins begin to colour and they soften. Remove the skins, then cut out the tough core and cut the flesh into quarters.

Remove the skin from the cooled pepper, then deseed it and slice the flesh into strips. Cut the courgette/zucchini into slices that are slightly thicker than the aubergine/eggplant, season with salt and brush with oil. Also brush both sides of the dried aubergine/eggplant slices with oil and put both the sliced vegetables under the grill/broiler. Cook until tender, turning once, brushing with olive oil if required. Remove from the grill/broiler and allow to cool before cutting into strips of roughly the same width as the pepper.

Combine the vegetables in a large bowl, then stir through the fresh herbs. Dress with a little more salt, pepper and oil.

Preheat the oven to 100°C (200°F) Gas ½ and put a plate in to warm. Remove the monkfish from the marinade and drain off any excess marinade. Heat a little oil in a non-stick frying pan over medium heat and fry the fish for 4–5 minutes on each side until they are just cooked and have developed a good colour. Remove from the frying pan and put on the warmed plate in the oven for 4–5 minutes to rest.

To serve, put a monkfish fillet on the plate and arrange the grilled vegetable salad alongside. Dress the fish with a few teaspoons of the Antillais Caper and Scotch Bonnet Sauce. This is also excellent served with plain rice and peas.

Crab, Lime and Scotch Bonnet Sauce

I love this French Caribbean sauce. It takes a few of my favourite flavours and combines them to make a delicious and slightly unusual sauce. Crab seems to have been created to go with hot chillies, which in turn love to be combined with lime juice and coconut milk. This sauce is perfect for dressing fresh fish fillets that have been lightly grilled/broiled and is also remarkably good with a salad, especially egg and avocado.

1 tablespoon groundnut oil

1 onion, finely chopped

2 garlic cloves, finely chopped

1 Scotch Bonnet chilli, deseeded and finely chopped

1 carrot, finely chopped

50 ml/scant ¼ cup lime juice (juice of 1½–2 limes)

about 2 tablespoons coconut milk

175-g/6-oz. can white crab meat, drained (120 g/4¼ oz. drained weight)

1 teaspoon paprika

1 teaspoon thyme leaves

1 teaspoon rosemary leaves, finely chopped

a small handful of chives

sea salt and freshly ground black pepper

Heat the oil in a medium saucepan over medium heat and fry the onion for 5 minutes, or until it begins to colour and soften (do not let it burn). Add the garlic and chilli and fry for another 1–2 minutes, stirring to stop the ingredients sticking to the pan.

Add the carrot, lime juice and 2 tablespoons coconut milk. Stir to combine and bring to a gentle simmer. Add hot water or more coconut milk if the sauce is too dry. Stir in the crab meat, then simmer gently until the carrots are cooked. Stir in the paprika, thyme and rosemary, then remove from the heat. Using a blender or stick blender, blitz the mixture to an even but still slightly coarse-textured sauce. Snip the chives into the sauce and stir through. Season to taste with salt and pepper.

This sauce is great served from the pan on warm foods such as grilled/broiled fish or transferred to an airtight container and placed in the fridge to chill to room temperature to be used as a salad dressing. This will keep for several days, sealed, in the fridge.

I would use this: in a white sauce to pep up a fish pie or with a potato salad.

Caribbean Black Bean and Mango Salsa

This is a fantastic alternative to the kind of "regular" salsas that we always see served with nachos. This recipe is somewhere around medium heat and is perfect for a family barbecue. If you want to up the heat a little, I would recommend using a finely diced fiery Scotch Bonnet or Habanero chilli and maybe using a dry jerk seasoning in the place of the Cajun spice.

400-g/14-oz. can black beans, rinsed and drained

1 small mango, finely chopped

1 small red onion, chopped

1 small hot fresh chilli, deseeded and very finely chopped

1 small green sweet/bell pepper, deseeded and chopped

2 plum tomatoes, deseeded and chopped

juice of 1 small lime

1 tablespoon cider vinegar

½ teaspoon garlic salt

½ teaspoon Cajun spice blend

½ teaspoon cayenne pepper

a small handful of coriander/cilantro, chopped

Put the beans in a medium bowl with the mango, onion, chilli, sweet/bell pepper, tomatoes, lime juice and vinegar. Turn them gently together to avoid breaking up the individual pieces of fruit and veg.

Season with the garlic salt, Cajun spice blend and cayenne pepper and carefully mix through, making sure that everything is evenly covered. Just before serving, add the coriander/cilantro and stir gently to combine.

I would use this: as a great dip for nachos or as a summer-barbecue salsa.

Hot Chilli Coconut Dip

This is a hot and exotic dip that brings together creamy coconut, fruity mango and devilishly hot chillies in an original and surprising dip. Adding the hot oil to the fresh ingredients just takes the edge off their raw flavours without cooking them. Ensure that all the ingredients are really well mixed together before refrigerating so that every mouthful contains sweet, sour, herby and hot flavours.

1 tablespoon vegetable oil

3 Habanero chillies, (ideally Trinidad Congo, Antillais Caribbean, Orange Habanero), deseeded and finely chopped

2 large spring onions/scallions, thinly sliced

2 garlic cloves, crushed

½ teaspoon thyme leaves

1 teaspoon salt

250 ml/1 cup coconut milk

50 g/1¾ oz. ripe avocado, mashed

50 g/1¾ oz. mango, cut into 1-cm/½-inch dice

1 tablespoon cider vinegar

zest and juice of 1 lime

coriander/cilantro and freshly ground black pepper, to garnish (optional)

Heat the oil in a small saucepan over medium heat until hot. Put the chillies, onions, garlic, thyme leaves and salt in a small heatproof bowl and pour the hot oil over. Stir as the oil cools a little, then pour off the excess oil.

Clean the pan and pour in the coconut milk, then add the avocado, mango and vinegar. Bring to the boil, stirring frequently. As the first bubbles appear, remove the pan from the heat and pour over the chilli mixture from the bowl. Stir well, then allow to cool a little and add the lime zest and juice. Refrigerate until required. To serve, add chopped coriander/cilantro and black pepper, if you like.

I would use this: as a dip for barbecued chicken or veggie kebabs/kabobs.

Prime Minister Errol Barrow's Hot Chilli Sauce

Errol Barrow was Prime Minister of Barbados, not once but twice. Among his many feats, including being a World War II fighter pilot and a successful barrister (and, of course, Prime Minister) he also produced a cookbook. "Privilege: Cooking in the Caribbean" was published in 1988 a year after he died. This was his favourite recipe for hot sauce.

12 large Scotch Bonnet chillies, deseeded and chopped

2 onions, roughly chopped

5 small garlic cloves, chopped

2 tablespoons English mustard

2 tablespoons white wine vinegar

2 tablespoons vegetable oil

2 large carrots, finely chopped

sea salt and freshly ground black pepper

Put the chillies in a saucepan over medium heat and add the onions, garlic, mustard, vinegar, oil and carrots. Measure out 400 ml/1¾ cups water. Add 200 ml/¾ cup water and bring to the boil, stirring frequently. Allow to boil for 15–20 minutes, adding more water if the contents begin to dry out. Blend all the ingredients using a stick blender or mini food processor to make a smooth purée. Return to the pan and season to taste with the salt and pepper. Adjust the consistency by adding more water if required. Return to the boil and immediately pour into sterilized jars, then seal. Allow to cool and store in the fridge.

I would use this: as a table condiment for any meat, fish or vegetable dish. This is a classic Bajan hot sauce. It contains no sugar, but you may wish to add 1 tablespoon with the water to slightly sweeten the finished sauce.

Adobo Mojado

An "adobo" was the original Spanish means of preserving meat. Today, it is a favourite marinade for meat and fish in Spanish-speaking Central American and Caribbean countries.

6–8 garlic cloves, crushed

2 tablespoons paprika (or
    1 tablespoon each paprika
    and Ancho chilli powder)

1 tablespoon salt

1 tablespoon dried oregano

1 green Jalapeño chilli,
    deseeded and chopped

125 ml/½ cup vegetable oil

50 ml/scant ¼ cup cider vinegar

2 tablespoons lime or orange
    juice, or a mixture of both

1 teaspoon brown sugar

½ teaspoon ground cumin

Put all the ingredients in a food processor and blend to a smooth paste. Store in a sealed jar in the fridge until you are ready to use. I would keep this paste for a week before using it to allow the flavours to mingle, merge and improve.

I would use this: to marinate any meat, fish or seafood dish before cooking. See also below.

Traditional Roast Chicken in Adobo Mojado (opposite)

I love cooking Sunday lunch – and also feel very fortunate to have an eight-year-old son who loves to cook and particularly enjoys peeling potatoes and carrots, which is my least favourite task. This recipe is for our family favourite of roast chicken – but with a little Puerto Rican twist.

2 kg/4½ lbs. free-range organic
    chicken, enough for 6 people

Adobo Mojado (see above)

1 large or 2 small lemons,
    pricked all over with a sharp
    knife

a handful of mixed herbs
    (thyme, bay, rosemary,
    tarragon)

about 60 g/4 tablespoons
    butter, softened

sea salt and freshly ground
    black pepper

Put the chicken in a roasting pan. Rub the Adobo Mojado over the chicken both inside and out. Try to work it under the skin as well, so that the flavour can penetrate the meat. If necessary, make a few slits in the skin using a very sharp knife. Cover and marinate in the fridge for at least 2 hours.

Preheat the oven to 220°C (425°F) Gas 7.

Uncover the chicken and put the lemons and herbs in the cavity. Add a generous knob of butter. Coat the outside of the chicken with more butter and sprinkle with a little salt and pepper. Pour a little water into the base of the roasting pan, cover the chicken with foil and put in the oven.

After 10 minutes, reduce the temperature to 200°C (400°F) Gas 6 and cook for 1 hour 10 minutes, basting twice with the liquid from the pan. About halfway through cooking, remove the foil to allow the skin to brown. The chicken is cooked when the juices run clear: test by inserting a skewer into the thickest part of the meat. If necessary, return to the oven for another 10 minutes and test again. Put on a serving dish, cover with foil and a tea towel, and set aside to rest for 15 minutes before carving. Serve with roast potatoes and vegetables. Put the roasting pan over the heat and cook to reduce the juices to serve with the chicken.

Noted Chillies: Piment D'Espelette, Pimentón (paprika – pictured here, right), Peperoncini, Bulgarian Carrot (pictured here, left), Hungarian Hot Wax.

Chilli Facts and Fiction: Calabria in Italy is home to the world's only chilli pepper museum: the Museo del Peperoncino.

Chapter Four

Mediterranean

Historically the Mediterranean was the first place outside the Americas to be "colonized" by chillies; however they were not readily adopted into European cuisines, and it was some time later, when chillies spread back from India along the spice trail, that they finally made their impact in Europe. When Christopher Columbus first encountered chillies in the Caribbean, he confused their hot flavour with that of black pepper, hence the name "peppers".

- The European climate means that chillies can be grown only in limited areas, the Mediterranean coastline being one, although even here winters are too cold to allow the chilli plants to regularly survive all year without protection. When they were first brought to Portugal and Spain in the 16th century, chillies were cultivated in the monastic gardens and, although the monks cooked with them, they viewed the fruits as more of a seasoning – an alternative to black pepper (which was astonishingly expensive) – rather than a flavour in their own right.

- Spain produces the largest amount of chillies in Europe, although by global standards this is still a tiny amount; Spain does not even rank in the top-ten chilli producers. Spanish cuisine makes great use of paprika in all its forms, but makes very little use of the hotter varieties it grows for export. This is especially surprising because it was the Spanish who established chillies as central to the cuisine of the southern USA.

Rouille

This delicious French chilli pick-me-up is a recipe that I seem to remember knowing forever. I have no idea when or where I tried it first, but I travelled regularly in the South of France in the past and particularly during the late autumn. I pretty quickly became a fan of bouillabaisse (the classic fish soup). Rouille is often employed to give this classic a little kick. I loved the warming chilli hit, especially when eaten outside in the last few days of autumn sunshine.

1 slice of stale white bread, crusts removed

1 red sweet/bell pepper, roasted, peeled and roughly chopped (page 83)

2 plump garlic cloves, roughly chopped

a good glug of fine olive oil

2 medium-heat red chillies, deseeded and chopped

sea salt and freshly ground black pepper

Soak the bread in a little water to soften it for a few minutes. Squeeze out the excess water and combine the bread with the sweet/bell pepper and the other ingredients.

Using a blender or food processor, blend the mixture until you have a smooth paste. Season with salt and pepper to taste. Transfer to a serving bowl and set aside until you are ready to use it.

I would use this: added to a bowl of simple fish soup (a spoonful or two of Rouille), or even Spanish garlic soup after serving.

Mediterranean Seasoning Rub

Although I originally put together this rub to be used with poultry and fish, it has subsequently become one of my favourite mixes for adding depth of flavour to all kinds of recipes. It's a lovely additional flavouring for tomato sauces or soups and a key ingredient in my partridge and white bean casserole.

4 tablespoons sweet paprika

1 teaspoon cayenne pepper

2 teaspoons dried thyme

1 teaspoon dried marjoram

1 teaspoon dried lavender

2 teaspoons soft brown sugar

1 teaspoon dried onion powder

½ teaspoon garlic powder

½ teaspoon sea salt

½ teaspoon freshly ground black pepper

1 bay leaf, ground

Put all the ingredients in a large sealable jar and shake well to combine evenly. Transfer to a sterilized jar and seal. This will keep for several months in a cool dark place before it loses its zip.

I would use this: for all poultry. It's great to mix with a little olive oil and a squeeze of lemon juice to make it into a paste and then rub it onto chicken before roasting.

Rosemary and Chilli-infused Vinegar

I love to make this with sherry vinegar and use it to deglaze roasted dishes. The rosemary flavouring works fantastically well with roast lamb and, when mixed with the roasting juices, provides a great base for a rich gravy or reduced sauce.

2 dried rosemary sprigs (see method for drying)

6 small dried red chillies, such as tiny, hot Zimbabwe Bird chillies

500 ml/2 cups good-quality wine vinegar or sherry vinegar

2 garlic cloves, unpeeled, pierced several times using a cocktail stick/toothpick or sharp knife

If you need to dry your rosemary and chillies, the simplest way to do this is to put them on a baking sheet in an oven preheated to 70°C (150°F) Gas ¼. Leave the door slightly ajar to allow the moisture to evaporate from the fruit and herbs. The rosemary and chillies should still maintain a little flexibility after drying. If they are completely desiccated they will fall to pieces in the vinegar. Drying the flavourings means that the only moisture left in them will be the flavour-rich oils that we want to transfer into the vinegar.

Sterilize 2 × 250 ml/1 cup bottles with tight seals. In a large saucepan, heat the vinegar over medium heat until it just begins to boil, then add the chillies and garlic. Reduce the heat and gently simmer for 5 minutes.

Push one rosemary sprig into each bottle. Divide the chillies and garlic evenly between the bottles and immediately pour the hot vinegar into the bottles leaving at least a 2-cm/¾-inch air gap at the top. Seal tightly and shake. Allow to cool naturally and put in a cool, dark place to infuse for at least 2 weeks or preferably up to 2 months. Turn the bottles regularly to aid infusion.

I would use this: to make salad dressings, in tomato sauces, to deglaze roasting dishes or to make quick vegetable pickles.

Super-speedy Patatas Bravas Sauce

Here is a great way to get all those delicious smoky, tomatoey Spanish flavours on the table in no time. It's ideal as a dip or as a speedy treat. Add some 1-cm/½-inch cubes of chorizo when you are frying the onions and you'll have an impromptu, but delicious, pasta sauce.

2 tablespoons olive oil

1 onion, finely chopped

2 garlic cloves, crushed

225 g/8 oz. passata (Italian sieved tomatoes)

1 teaspoon paprika

½ teaspoon spicy smoked paprika (Pimentón Piccante)

1 tablespoon red wine vinegar

a good pinch of sea salt

a pinch of sugar

1 teaspoon dried oregano

chopped flat leaf parsley

Heat the oil in a medium saucepan over medium heat. Add the onion and fry for 2–3 minutes. Add the garlic and fry for a further 1 minute.

Pour in the passata. Add the paprikas, vinegar, salt, sugar and oregano. Stir thoroughly, then turn up the heat and bring the mixture to the boil. Reduce the heat and simmer for a further 5 minutes, stirring regularly. Add the parsley, mix well and serve.

I would use this: as a dip for fried potatoes or wedges – a kind of Spanish ketchup.

Perfect Spanish Seasoning Paste

Early mornings are an abiding memory of all my trips to Spain – taking photographs as the sun rose, and now loving being at the market with the locals getting everything fresh from the fields. This recipe is a distillation of all those fresh ingredients, spices and colours. The essence of Spain in tastes and smells!

a few saffron threads

50 ml/scant ¼ cup warmed fish stock or water

1 tablespoon olive oil

4 shallots, finely chopped

4 garlic cloves, finely chopped

1 tablespoon sherry vinegar

2 tablespoons tomato purée/paste

1 teaspoon vegetable bouillon powder

1 teaspoon Pimentón Dulce

½ teaspoon Pimentón Piccante

½ teaspoon dried chilli flakes

a small handful of flat leaf parsley, finely chopped

sea salt and freshly ground black pepper

Put the saffron in a small bowl and add the stock. Allow to infuse/steep for 20–30 minutes. Meanwhile, heat a medium frying pan over a medium-low heat, add the oil and shallots and cook for 5 minutes, or until they begin to soften. Add the garlic and cook, stirring frequently, until the onions are soft. Add the vinegar, tomato purée/paste, bouillon powder, both types of paprika and the chilli flakes. Mix well and add the saffron-infused stock. Cook over low heat for 3 minutes, stirring frequently.

Pour the mixture into a blender or mini food processor and pulse to a smooth paste. Season with salt and pepper, then add the parsley. Blend briefly to mix. The paste should be thick, glossy and smooth. If it is too thick, add a little boiled water or warmed stock, and blend again. If the paste is a little loose, return it to the pan and gently cook, stirring constantly, until the mixture reduces. The paste will thicken a little when it cools. Pack immediately into a sterilized jar and cool then refrigerate.

I would use this: to flavour Bomba or Arborio rice dishes; as a base for a chorizo and seafood stew; in a tasty, quick monkfish paella.

Salsa Verde Piccante

It pains me to say it but I have never been a "green" fan: pea purée, broad/fava bean salad, all those fresh spring flavours seem to leave me rather cold – on their own that is. My palate always hankers for some robustness somewhere. Combining the deliciousness of parsley, basil and mint with capers and with lemon, garlic and anchovy changes everything for me.

a handful of flat leaf parsley, chopped

a small handful of basil, torn

a few mint leaves, chopped

2–3 tablespoons capers

zest of 1 lemon

1 small hot green chilli, deseeded and finely chopped

6 anchovy fillets, drained, rinsed, dried and chopped

1 garlic clove, crushed

1 hot green chilli, deseeded and very finely chopped

1 tablespoon extra virgin olive oil, or as needed

sea salt and freshly ground black pepper

Put all the ingredients into a large mortar and mash to a rough paste using a pestle. Alternatively, put all the ingredients into a food processor and pulse briefly for a few seconds. Loosen with extra olive oil as required and season with a little salt and pepper.

This salsa is wonderfully robust so don't be afraid to experiment with the herbs used. If you have a glut of one herb, throw it in! My own favourite variations use freshly picked wild garlic leaves or garden-grown French tarragon.

I would use this: to serve with fish or to stuff a fish you are roasting; with smoked salmon as a bold filling for canapés.

Marinade for Pinchitos Morunos

Pinchitos Morunos is a classic Andalusian tapas dish. The name actually translates literally to "Moorish Spikes". Pork, lamb or chicken is marinated in this spicy sauce before being skewered and cooked, traditionally on a wood-fired barbecue. Tapas has to be the most exciting way to get children to try new foods that in any other circumstance they would firmly believe they didn't like. On their first trip to Spain, both my older boys discovered that they actually loved squid, which they would never have tried at home.

a few saffron threads

1 teaspoon sweet smoked
    paprika (Pimentón Dulce)

½ teaspoon sea salt

½ teaspoon coriander seeds

½ teaspoon ground cumin

½ teaspoon fennel seeds

1 teaspoon dried oregano

1 bay leaf, central stalk
    discarded, finely chopped

2 garlic cloves, finely chopped

2 teaspoons sherry vinegar

2 teaspoons olive oil

Put the saffron in a small jar and add 2 tablespoons hot water. Allow to infuse/steep for 20 minutes.

Put the paprika, salt, coriander, cumin, fennel, oregano and bay in a bowl and mix together. Add the garlic, vinegar, oil and the saffron liquid. Stir thoroughly. Transfer to a sterilized glass jar and seal tightly. This will keep in the fridge for several weeks.

I would use this: to marinate pork, lamb or chicken. See also below.

Pinchitos Morunos "Moorish Spikes" (opposite)

This recipe is made to be barbecued — over a wood fire, obviously. I fail to grasp how a gas barbecue differs from conventional cooking in the kitchen, since it adds nothing to the flavour of any dish. If you can't appreciate the value of a real fire, cook them on a griddle or under a hot grill/broiler!

500 g/1 lb. 2 oz. free-range
    skinless and boneless
    chicken thigh meat, cut into
    2.5-cm/1-inch cubes

Marinade for Pinchitos Morunos
    (see above)

a dressed tomato and parsley
    salad, and fresh bread to
    serve

4 metal skewers (or wooden
    ones, soaked for 2 hours)

Serves 4 as a tapas dish or with salad
and bread for a light lunch

Put the diced chicken in a large bowl. Add the marinade and rub into the chicken ensuring that each piece is thoroughly coated. Pack into a small container with a tightly fitting lid and put in the fridge to marinate for 2–3 hours.

Prepare a barbecue. Slide the chicken onto the skewers ensuring it is snugly pressed together to form a continuous kebab/kabob of chicken.

Cook over fairly high heat until the chicken is cooked through but still juicy on the inside. Serve with a light tomato and parsley salad, dressed with freshly squeezed lemon juice and good olive oil and fresh bread.

Boozy Berry Tirami-ifle

Anyone who knows me will tell you that I simply don't eat desserts. The exception to this is a berry cheesecake, quality trifle or tiramisu, so why not combine all three in a single dish? With the added delight of espresso coffee and liqueur digestifs, this entire creation is a veritable riot of excess, alcohol, fun and flavour.

4–6 Savoiardi biscuits or trifle sponges, roughly broken

Spiced Conserva Antica (page 76)

50 g/1¾ oz. dark/bittersweet chocolate

250 g/9 oz. fresh vanilla custard, warmed

150 ml/scant ⅔ cup whipping cream

125 g/½ cup mascarpone cheese

1 tablespoon clear honey

1 teaspoon unsweetened cocoa powder

espresso coffee, to serve

Serves 4–6

Divide the biscuits and among 4 wine glasses, then add 2 tablespoons of the boozy berry mixture from the Spiced Conserva Antica to each glass (reserve about 4 tablespoons of the liqueur). Allow to stand to absorb the syrup while you make the chocolate custard.

Break up 40 g/1½ oz. of the chocolate into a heatproof bowl over a pan of gently simmering water, making sure that the base doesn't touch the water. Allow the chocolate to melt, then remove from the heat and stir in the warmed custard. Allow to cool.

In a separate bowl, whip together the cream, mascarpone and honey until light and fluffy. Very carefully fold in the reserved liqueur syrup from the berries.

Divide half the mascarpone and cream mixture between the 4 glasses, then divide the chocolate custard between the glasses too. Top each glass with a final layer of mascarpone mixture. Sculpt to an elegant peak before placing in the fridge to chill.

Sift the cocoa powder and grate the remaining chocolate over the top. Return to the fridge until you are ready to serve. Serve with an espresso coffee. Put a jar of Spiced Conserva Antica on the table with a miniature ladle and encourage your guests to refill their espresso cups with the fruity berry liqueur.

Spiced Conserva Antica

If I had to recommend a great weekend away if you love food (and frankly, if you don't, you have picked up the wrong book), near the top of my list would be Salone del Gusto in Turin – the Italian biennial celebration of slow food. The 12-hour days take the art of "grazing" to a new level, but if you have any space left, the cuisine of the surrounding Piedmont area is a delight. We had stopped in Ivrea and, after a quite delicious lunch of pasta with walnut sauce for me and pasta with wild mushrooms for my wife, we were just finishing the requisite espresso when a huge jar of Conserva Antica was placed on our table with a miniature ladle. After a few moments of spying on other diners, we realized that you ladle the fruity liqueur into your coffee cup. I can't recommend this highly enough. The berries and the alcohol combine wonderfully with the hint of coffee from the foam left in the cup – it's the perfect end to any meal.

2.5 kg/5½ lbs. assorted fruits, such as raspberries, blueberries, blackberries, redcurrants, blackcurrants (cherries and apples also work very well)

1 dried Pasilla chilli, deseeded and cut into short strips

2 litres/8¾ cups aquavit (or brandy, cognac, rum, good vodka, grappa, etc.)

1 kg/5 cups sugar

½ teaspoon freshly grated nutmeg

½ teaspoon ground cinnamon

Rinse the fruit and allow to dry. Remove the stones and cores as necessary and peel the fruit if required. Cut the berries, currants and cherries in half and slice the apple. Put the fruit and chilli strips in layers in a sterilized storage jar and cover with the alcohol. Seal tightly and give the contents a really good shake. Put somewhere cool, dark and dry for about a week, giving the jar an occasional shake if you remember!

Put the sugar and 150 ml/⅔ cup water in a saucepan over medium heat and slowly bring to the boil, stirring regularly, to ensure that the sugar dissolves and doesn't burn or stick. Allow to cool, then pour into the jar with the fruit and alcohol mixture. Add the nutmeg and cinnamon, stir well and reseal the jar. Return it to its cool, dark resting place and leave for at least a month.

I would use this: to serve with chocolate tortes, cheesecake or even ice cream – the larger pieces of fruit are ideal for this. The syrup and the smaller fruits are wonderful with coffee as described above and the syrup makes a lovely liqueur. It can also be packed into smaller decorative bottles or jars as a great Christmas present! See also page 74.

Mostarda Mantovana

Having first been committed to paper (or possibly parchment) as early as the 13th century, this classic recipe from the Angevin Court seems to be one of the earliest mustard recipes recorded. It is certainly the earliest I have seen that is still made in the same way today. By the 15th century, it was already more famous in Italy than in Anjou where it appears to have begun its life. It is now universally associated with the Lombardy region of northern Italy and is wonderful with the classic "tortelli di zucca" (pumpkin ravioli).

1 kg/2¼ lbs. quinces (or sharp, firm-fleshed and slightly underripe apples or pears), peeled, cored and sliced

500 g/2½ cups sugar

3 tablespoons white wine

50 g/1¾ oz. yellow/white mustard seeds, ground (or 50 g/1¾ oz. mustard powder)

Put the quinces in a large bowl, add the sugar and mix thoroughly. Cover and set aside for 24 hours.

Pour off the juices into a heavy-based saucepan over medium heat and bring to the boil, stirring. Reduce the heat and simmer for 10 minutes, or until slightly reduced. Return these juices to the fruit bowl and mix thoroughly again. Cover and set aside for a further 24 hours.

Repeat this process, this time bringing the juices to a very gentle simmer for 5 minutes, and then set aside for another 24 hours.

Pour the sugar syrup and the fruit into the pan over medium heat and gently reheat. Then reduce the heat and simmer for 5–10 minutes until the fruit is just softened. Remove the pan from the heat.

Gently warm the white wine in a small saucepan and stir in the ground mustard to make a smooth paste. Add this to the fruit mixture and mix well. Transfer immediately to sterilized glass jars and seal tightly. Store in a cool, dark place until needed. It will keep for many months.

I would use this: to accompany boiled meats or with cheese.

Sofrito

In many ways Sofrito is the basis of Spanish cooking, but it exists in a variety of forms throughout the Mediterranean, the Caribbean and Central America, often using more garlic or plenty of green peppers, lots more chilli or no chilli at all. The essence of the dish is in the way the ingredients are cooked in oil rather than stewed in water. Because of this you are able to cook it more quickly and at a higher heat. This seems to intensify the individual flavours as well as melding them together into something that definitely exceeds the sum of its parts. A classic Spanish Sofrito would have no additional chilli beyond the paprika, although the fruity Piquillo chilli is not out of place, adding a delicious zip to the sauce. The option of including some Habanero chilli adds a little punch to the classic recipe.

4 tablespoons good-quality olive oil (the choice of oil has a great effect on the final flavour so use the best oil you can, with a flavour you like)

1 large onion, finely chopped

2 garlic cloves, finely chopped

1 large red sweet/bell pepper, deseeded and finely chopped

3 Piquillo chillies, finely chopped

½ Habanero chilli, deseeded and finely chopped (optional)

4 large ripe plum tomatoes, peeled, deseeded and chopped

1 fresh bay leaf

1 thyme sprig

½ teaspoon paprika

sea salt and freshly ground black pepper

Heat a heavy-based saucepan over medium heat and add the oil. Add the onion and fry, stirring regularly, until it turns golden brown and caramelized. It is very important not to allow the onion to burn or stick to the pan, but it is equally important to ensure the heat is high enough to cook it evenly.

Add the garlic, bell/sweet pepper and chillies and fry for 3–4 minutes until they soften without over-browning. Add the tomatoes, bay leaf and thyme and cook for a further 15 minutes, stirring frequently. Stir in the paprika and cook for 5 minutes. Remove from the heat and season well with salt and pepper to taste. Remove the bay leaf and the thyme sprig.

I would use this: as the perfect sauce for homemade pizza. It can also be used as a delicious substitute for regular tomato purée/paste in any dish. See also opposite.

Fra Diavolo Sauce

Calabria is the biggest producer (and consumer) of chillies in Italy, and their food contains peperoncini at every turn. We commonly find Calabrian Ciliegia chillies stuffed with cheese or anchovies sold as antipasti in the UK. The Calabrians are also legendary for their "salsa piccante". This sauce is a great way to use up any glut of fresh chillies and can be made to suit any palate. It can be added to some fresh tomatoes to make a fantastic "all'arrabiata" sauce for pasta. Fra Diavolo literally translates as "Brother Devil".

2 tablespoons olive oil

3 shallots, finely chopped

4–5 garlic cloves, crushed

2 Peperone red sweet/bell peppers (or Romano), finely chopped

100 g/3½ oz. mixed red chillies, such as Ciliega, Naso di Cane and Amando or Cherry Bomb, Red Jalapeño and Ring of Fire cayenne, finely chopped

3 tablespoons red wine vinegar

2 tablespoons tomato purée/paste (or Sofrito – see opposite)

1 teaspoon dried oregano

1 teaspoon sea salt, or to taste

freshly ground black pepper

Heat the oil in a heavy-based saucepan over medium-low heat. Add the shallots and fry gently for 5 minutes, or until they soften. Add the garlic, sweet/bell peppers and chillies and continue to gently fry for 10 minutes.

Add the vinegar, tomato purée/paste and oregano, then stir well and allow to gently simmer for another 20 minutes, adding a little water if the consistency becomes too dry. Season with salt and pepper to taste. The sauce can be blended into a smoother consistency, if you like, or stored in a sterilized jar as a chunky paste.

I would use this: as the basis for a great seafood sauce served with fresh pasta.

Mallorcan Romescu Sauce (opposite)

During a spring break to Mallorca we spent most of the week cooking all our food in a huge traditional wood-fired oven. It took many hours and piles of wood, but the flavour of the food was superb. I was served this sauce in a bar in Pollensa alongside grilled/broiled fish. This is exactly how it was made, using oven-roasted ingredients. You can use Pimentón Piccante if you prefer a smoky, hotter flavour.

5 large ripe vine-ripened tomatoes

1 large garlic bulb

100 g/3½ oz. toasted almonds, finely chopped

1 teaspoon dried chilli flakes

125 ml/½ cup good-quality extra virgin olive oil

1 tablespoon sweet paprika, or to taste

1–2 tablespoons sherry vinegar, preferably Jerez sherry vinegar

½ teaspoon sea salt, or to taste

Wrap each tomato and the bulb of garlic individually in foil. Roast in a hot wood-fired oven (or in a regular oven preheated to 200°C (400°F) Gas 6, or directly on the embers of your barbecue). Peel the tomatoes and put in a large mortar. Squeeze the roasted garlic cloves out of their skins into the mortar. Start to work these together using a pestle.

Add the almonds, chilli, oil and paprika. Work together to form a fairly coarse but well mixed paste. Add the vinegar and salt according to taste. You can also add more paprika, if you like.

I would use this: with fish or meat or as a dip for the traditional Mallorcan nibble of spring onions/scallions lightly charred over the fire.

Sherry Vinegar and Smoked Paprika Marinade

Here is a lovely southern Spanish marinade with Moorish overtones of cumin and lemon. We first made this recipe in the hills outside Ronda, Andalusia. We scored a leg of lamb and marinated it for several hours in this blend and then roasted it in a hot oven, with potatoes roasted in the fat from the meat.

2 tablespoons sherry vinegar

3 tablespoons olive oil

2 garlic cloves, crushed

1 teaspoon cumin seeds

2 teaspoons coarse sea salt

1 teaspoon hot smoked paprika (Pimentón Piccante)

1 teaspoon sweet smoked paprika (Pimentón Dulce)

1 dried bay leaf, central stalk discarded, finely chopped

1 teaspoon rosemary leaves, finely chopped

zest and juice from ½ lemon

Pour the vinegar and oil into a bowl. Add the garlic and whisk together. Put the cumin seeds and salt in a mortar and use a pestle to crush them lightly together.

Tip the cumin-seed mixture into the bowl with the garlic, and add the hot and sweet paprikas, the herbs, and lemon zest and juice. Mix thoroughly together.

I would use this: as a marinade for lamb and chicken before roasting, or even with mackerel.

My Favourite Jordanian Baharat Blend (opposite: left)

When I was 14, my parents decided it would be a good idea to broaden my horizons and encourage me to explore some of the more accessible parts of the Middle East, so we set off in October 1985 for a short but eventful tour. Many years later, when I discovered the heady aromas of freshly ground Baharat (which, incidentally, is simply Arabic for "spice"), it immediately took me back to that trip and the wonderfully fragrant aubergine/eggplant and lentil stews I had eaten. It also reminded me of my first taste of "arak", the fiery aniseed spirit seemingly drunk by everyone in the region – at 14 I was definitely considered adult, even if (I have to admit) my constitution turned out not to be.

1 tablespoon red peppercorns

1 tablespoon mixed peppercorns (black, green and white)

1½ tablespoons coriander seeds

1½ tablespoons cumin seeds

½ tablespoon allspice berries

2 teaspoons cloves

½ tablespoon cardamom pods

½ tablespoon grated nutmeg

4 tablespoons sweet paprika

½ teaspoon ground cinnamon

1 teaspoon dried chilli flakes

Put the peppercorns in a heavy-based saucepan over medium heat and add the coriander seeds, cumin seeds, allspice berries, cloves and cardamom pods. Lightly toast the seeds, tossing the pan regularly. Remove from the heat and allow to cool. Remove the cardamom seeds from the toasted pods and discard the empty pods.

Put all the ingredients in a mortar, and combine using a pestle until you have a fairly fine and even grind. (Alternatively, use a food processor or grinder.) The blend will smell fantastic. I use it as an integral part of my own Astonishingly Aromatic Moroccan Tagine Paste (page 30). Transfer to an airtight container and store in a cool, dark place. It will happily keep for several months if stored in this way.

I would use this: for cooking lentils, aubergine/eggplant, lamb, chicken and venison. See also page 30.

Za'atar Spice Blend (opposite: middle)

This blend is a tasty variation on the Za'atar theme. It's a herb and sesame combination that works surprisingly well as a topping for sweet or savoury dishes, and it's great as an alternative to dukkah.

2 teaspoons sesame seeds

2 teaspoons dried oregano

2 teaspoons ground sumac

3 teaspoons thyme leaves, finely chopped (use wild thyme, if you can get it)

1 teaspoon sea salt

1½ teaspoons ground cumin

Put the sesame seeds in a small saucepan over medium heat and toast for 2 minutes, or until they begin to brown. Remove from the heat and put half the seeds in a blender with the other ingredients and pulse for 10–20 seconds. Tip into a bowl and stir in the remaining sesame seeds. Store in an airtight jar in the fridge for up to 1 week.

I would use this: to sprinkle on hummus, cooked meat or vegetables. Or to finish a salad, or with fresh pitta bread to dip in olive oil and then to coat with the spice mix.

Muhammara (below: right)

Although a Syrian speciality, Muhammara is now popular throughout the Eastern Mediterranean. This spicy red pepper and walnut dip is served in much the same way as hummus. Use it to dip toasted strips of pitta bread or carrot sticks into, or serve it as a sauce for grilled/broiled meat and fish. Although pomegranate molasses might seem like a particularly unusual ingredient, it is readily available from a number of online healthfood stores if you can't get it at your local supermarket.

4 red sweet/bell peppers

1 teaspoon cumin seeds

100 g/⅔ cup walnuts

a good handful of fresh breadcrumbs

2–3 garlic cloves

1–2 tablespoons lemon juice

2 teaspoons pomegranate molasses

1 tablespoon dried chilli flakes

125 ml/½ cup extra virgin olive oil

sea salt and freshly ground black pepper

Spear the sweet/bell peppers onto a long fork or metal skewer and carefully fire-roast them over a naked flame, or put under a hot grill/broiler until the skins start to blacken and blister. Put the peppers in a plastic food bag and tie the top. Leave for 10 minutes, or until the skins to start to peel away from the flesh.

Meanwhile, put the cumin seeds in heavy-based saucepan over medium heat and lightly toast, tossing the pan frequently. Put them in a mortar and grind using the pestle. Toast the walnuts in the same way, then roughly chop them.

Remove the roasted peppers from the bag and peel, deseed and roughly chop the flesh. Put the peppers, ground cumin and chopped walnuts in a food processor and add the breadcrumbs, garlic, lemon juice, molasses, chilli flakes and oil. Blend to a smooth paste and season to taste with salt and pepper. Put in an airtight container and refrigerate until you are ready to use it. The flavours will continue to improve as they "mingle" if stored for a few days. It is always preferable to allow Muhammara to come to room temperature before serving.

I would use this: as a tasty alternative to hummus.

Noted Chillies: Serrano, Jalapeño, Chiltepin, Datil, Anaheim (pictured here, right), Santa Fe (pictured here, left), Cubanelle, Cascabel, Cayenne.

Chilli Facts and Fiction: In the Deep South, legend holds that in order to grow hot peppers you need to be angry when you plant them – the hottest peppers are by default thought to be grown by lunatics!

Chapter Five

USA

The USA is often now viewed as the home of chilli and hot sauces, but as a country its interest in spicy foods is relatively young. There have been areas that are influenced primarily by Mexican food, which embraced the use of chillies far sooner, but for most of the US the love of chillies has only really gathered pace since the mid 1970s.

- There have been many attempts to explain how and why this happened, but the overriding element in every theory is that as the ethnic diversity of America has increased (since World War II) so has the general acceptance of chillies and spicy foods. And as we see in other cultures, once you get to a second and third generation of chilli lovers there really is no turning back. You rarely hear of people who have grown up with richly spiced and flavoured foods craving plain boiled meat and potatoes!

- The US is undoubtedly the hot-sauce capital of the world. In 2012 hot sauce production was the eighth fastest growing industry in the country, driven by domestic demand and that of Canada and Japan. In the US alone there are about 50,000–60,000 acres of agricultural land in use for commercially grown hot peppers.

- The southernmost states of the US, particularly Arizona and Texas, are still home to the wild Chiltepin that spread up from northern Mexico. So proud are they of having the "mother" chilli in their state that Texas has made it its state plant. In Texas and New Mexico there are about 1000 acres of this essentially wild plant in cultivation.

Creole Rémoulade (below: left)

Rémoulade is a mighty, flavour-packed Louisiana-style mayonnaise heaving with big, bold flavours, so needless to say, I LOVE it. Creole food is influenced by European cooking, and it is this simple link that sets it apart from its Cajun neighbour. This recipe clearly illustrates the French connection. Rémoulade takes a classic mayonnaise and adds capers, shallots, tarragon, parsley and, of course, hot sauce. Adding finely chopped fresh chillies works excellently in this recipe.

2 large egg yolks

1 tablespoon Dijon mustard

250 ml/1 cup olive oil

1 teaspoon Tabasco or other Louisiana-style hot sauce

¼ teaspoon sea salt

a good pinch of freshly ground white pepper

1 tablespoon lemon juice

1 shallot, finely chopped

2 teaspoons capers, finely chopped

a very small bunch of tarragon

a few flat leaf parsley leaves

½ chilli, preferably Habanero, finely chopped (optional)

Put the egg yolks in a large mixing bowl and add the mustard. Whisk gently with a balloon whisk to break up the eggs and mix evenly. This is where it gets useful to have another pair of hands: briskly and evenly whisk the egg mixture while slowly adding the oil into the edge of the mixture in a thin ribbon – the slower this is added at the early stages the less likely the mayonnaise is to separate.

Once all the oil is blended, keep whisking and add the Tabasco, salt, pepper and lemon juice. Stir in the shallot, capers, tarragon, parsley and chilli (if using).

I would use this: to serve with fish and chips, or boiled new potatoes.

Louisiana Spicy Sauce (opposite: right)

This sauce is super-easy to make and cook with. My favourite way to use it has to be this Creole fish bake: pour the sauce over 2 firm-fleshed fish fillets in the morning, cover with foil and leave in the fridge; in the evening, roast the fish at 180°C (350°F) Gas 4 for 20–30 minutes or until it begins to flake with a fork.

15 g/1 tablespoon butter
1 onion, finely chopped
1 garlic clove, crushed
2 red sweet/bell peppers, deseeded and finely chopped
4 medium-heat chillies, deseeded and finely chopped
1 tablespoon red wine vinegar
400-g/14-oz. can chopped tomatoes
1 teaspoon sea salt
1 bay leaf
2 teaspoons dried thyme
½ teaspoon freshly ground black pepper
½ teaspoon cayenne pepper
¼ teaspoon ground cinnamon

Heat the butter in a heavy-based frying pan over medium heat and gently fry the onion for 2 minutes. Add the garlic and fry for a further 1 minute.

Add the red sweet/bell peppers and the chillies and fry for 3–4 minutes. Add the remaining ingredients, bring gently to the bowl, then reduce the heat and simmer for 45 minutes. Remove the bay leaf and allow to cool.

I would use this: as a marinade or cook-in-sauce for any meat or fish.

Cajun Blackening Spice

All you need to do to make this spice blend is add the ingredients to a jar and shake.

2 tablespoons dried thyme
1 tablespoon soft brown sugar
1 tablespoon sweet paprika
2 teaspoons dried onion powder
2 teaspoons freshly ground black pepper
1½ teaspoons sea salt
1 teaspoon garlic powder
1 teaspoon cayenne pepper
1 teaspoon dried oregano
¾ teaspoon ground cumin
½ teaspoon grated nutmeg
½ teaspoon ground allspice
2 bay leaves, central stalk discarded, finely chopped

Put all the ingredients in a sealable jar. Close the lid and shake until everything is evenly mixed. Store in a cool dark place until needed.

I would use this: mixed with a little flour as a coating for chicken or fish before frying or barbecuing.

Spicy Brown Roux for Gumbo (opposite, left)

A masterpiece of simplicity, this roux proves unquestionably that the answer to most questions is "more butter". Cajun food originated in Acadiana — the official name of the French Louisiana region at the southernmost point of the state. It lends itself to spicy, hearty one-pot dishes that make the most of the many vegetables and fruit that grow in the fertile soil in this area. It is also home to the beer method of measuring cooking times: for example, a 2-beer recipe needs to be cooked for the amount of time it takes to drink 2 beers. A good brown roux is definitely a 4-beer recipe — you have been warned!

275 g/2 sticks plus
   3 tablespoons salted butter

2 onions, finely chopped

4–5 garlic cloves, finely
   chopped

1 green sweet/bell pepper,
   deseeded and finely chopped

1 celery stick, finely chopped

4 medium-heat chillies, such as
   a mix of Jalapeño, Serrano,
   Cayenne and De Arbol, finely
   chopped

250 g/2 cups plain/all-purpose
   flour

Louisiana hot sauce, to taste

sea salt and freshly ground
   black pepper

Melt 25 g/2 tablespoons of the butter in a heavy-based saucepan over medium-low heat. Add the onions and fry very gently for 3 minutes, then add the garlic, green sweet/bell pepper and celery. Continue to fry gently until all the ingredients soften. Stir in the chillies, then fry for another 5 minutes over low heat. Transfer to a bowl and set aside.

Wipe out the pan and add the remaining butter. Reheat over medium heat until the butter melts. Slowly add the flour, a little at a time, stirring constantly. Be very careful to ensure that the roux mixture does not burn or catch on the pan (this would render it useless and you would need to start again). You should notice the flour beginning to brown. Keep stirring and cooking for 15 minutes, or until the roux takes on a rich, almost chocolate-brown colour. This is the perfect colour for making gumbo.

Add the reserved fried ingredients to the pan and stir them through the roux — be patient and try to ensure that everything is evenly mixed. Add seasoning and hot sauce to taste. Remove from the heat and allow to cool. Store in the fridge until required. It is good to make the roux in advance, as storing it will help the flavours to blend together.

I would use this: to make a major pot of chicken and smoked-sausage gumbo. See also page 90.

Zesty Cajun Seafood Sauce (right)

Again the "holy trinity" of Cajun cooking (celery, green sweet/bell pepper and onion) comes to the fore creating a classic flavour combination for this sauce, which is designed to smother on fish or seafood before cooking. For an interesting and entirely non-traditional twist, you can try substituting some smoky-flavoured Chipotle chillies that have been gently rehydrated in a little warm cider vinegar instead of using the fresh chillies. This combines brilliantly with the lime zest and juice.

4 tablespoons tomato purée/ paste

zest and juice of 1 lime

1 onion, finely chopped

½ celery stick, finely chopped

2 Jalapeño or Serrano chillies, finely chopped

½ green sweet/bell pepper, finely chopped

4 pitted green olives, finely chopped

1 tablespoon olive oil

1 teaspoon muscovado/ molasses sugar

a splash of Worcestershire sauce

sea salt and freshly ground black pepper

Combine all the ingredients in a bowl. Mix thoroughly and season with salt and pepper as required. Store in a tightly sealed jar in the fridge until you are ready to use it.

I would use this: to coat firm white fish or mixed seafood before cooking.

Louisiana Gumbo with Cajun Potato Salad

Cajun cuisine – gumbo, jambalaya, etouffee – is rich, delicious and satisfying. Each can be made using a combination of seafood, chicken, game, smoked meats, sausage and vegetables, and all are traditionally served with rice. For clarification, gumbo is a soup served with rice; jambalaya is a kind of distant cousin of paella where the rice is cooked in the stock with the other ingredients; etouffee is similar to gumbo but has a thicker sauce and is served as a main course/entrée spooned over rice, rather than as a soup.

This recipe is for the classic Louisiana chicken and smoked-sausage gumbo, but it also works beautifully with crab and prawns/shrimp, or rabbit and chorizo, and Tasso ham, a Cajun version of smoked pork shoulder, can also be added. A dollop of potato salad on top is the Cajun finish to the dish.

For the gumbo

2 tablespoons vegetable oil

about 1 kg/2¼ lbs. skinless, boneless chickens thighs, cut into large chunks

500 g/1 lb. 2 oz. Andouille sausage (or your preferred smoked sausage), thickly sliced

Spicy Brown Roux for Gumbo (page 88)

1 litre/4 cups warm chicken stock

200 g/7 oz. okra, roughly chopped

4 Jalapeño chillies, sliced in half lengthways and deseeded

a large handful of fresh parsley leaves, chopped

sea salt and freshly ground white pepper

For the Cajun potato salad

10 small waxy potatoes, unpeeled

1 tablespoon olive oil

juice of ½ lemon

1 celery stick, finely chopped

2 large mild green chillies, deseeded and roughly chopped

4 large spring onions/scallions, chopped

180 g/¾ cup mayonnaise

1 teaspoon Cajun spice blend

Serves 4

Gumbo

Heat the oil in a large heatproof casserole dish and fry the chicken and sausage until nicely browned. Remove from the pan and set aside.

Put the pan back over medium-low heat and add the Spicy Brown Roux. Gradually heat through, stirring as it softens. While stirring, gradually add enough stock to loosen the roux. Stir in about half the remaining stock and bring to a gentle simmer for 10 minutes. Add the chicken and sausage, the remaining stock, the okra and the Jalapeños. Stir together and simmer for 45 minutes–1 hour until cooked through, stirring regularly. Add more water or stock if required.

Cajun potato salad

Put the potatoes in a saucepan of lightly salted boiling water and boil for 15–20 minutes until cooked but still firm. Drain, then return the potatoes to the pan and add the olive oil and lemon juice. Cover with a lid and give the pan a good shake to coat the potatoes. Allow to cool with the lid on. Cut the potatoes into halves or quarters and put in a large bowl with the celery, chillies and onions. Add the mayonnaise and Cajun spice blend and gently combine together until well coated. Season with salt and pepper to taste.

Season the gumbo generously with salt and pepper, then stir in the chopped parsley. Serve in soup bowls with a generous spoonful of potato salad alongside or on the top, Cajun-style.

Dan's Roast Tomato, Garlic and Jalapeño Ketchup

It is a kindness of nature that the conditions where chillies thrive are also ideal for tomatoes. We always grow 4 or 5 different varieties: some small cherry tomatoes that are perfect in salads, still warm from the vine and loved by children; some heirloom Italian plum tomatoes for sauces; and some huge beefsteak tomatoes. Among these our favourite is the Black Russian – an enormous misshapen purpley black bowling-ball of a tomato. They are incredibly dense and have lots of tasty flesh with very little waste. I first made this recipe with these tomatoes and still love to do so whenever we have a glut. Unlike normal tomatoes, to make up to the 2 kg/4½ lbs. needed for the recipe we only need 4–5 of the Black Russian tomatoes; however, you do not need to make the sauce from a single variety of tomato and, in fact, using a good mix of varieties will result in a very balanced tomatoey flavour.

Base roast tomato sauce

For the base roast tomato sauce

2 kg/4½ lbs. very ripe tomatoes, halved

2–3 fresh bay leaves

2–3 thyme sprigs

2–3 tablespoons good-quality olive oil

1 garlic bulb

sea salt and freshly ground black pepper

triturator (optional)

Preheat the oven to 180°C (350°F) Gas 4. Put the halved tomatoes in a ceramic roasting dish, cut-side up. Pack them quite closely together so that they do not fall over. Push the bay and thyme in among the tomatoes, drizzle with the olive oil and season with salt and pepper.

Using a sharp knife, slice off the top of the garlic bulb, drizzle with olive oil and wrap in foil, creating a flat base so that the bulb will stand upright. Put this in the centre of the dish among the tomatoes. Roast for 45 minutes, or until the tomato skins have begun to char and the flesh has softened. Remove the foil-wrapped garlic and tip the remaining contents of the dish (including all the oil) into a triturator and turn the handle to separate the skin and seeds from the flesh. (Alternatively, rub the mixture through a sieve/strainer using the back of a spoon into a large bowl. Discard the seeds, skins and herbs.

Unwrap the garlic bulb and squeeze the flesh of each clove from its papery shell into the roasted tomato. Stir the roasted garlic flesh into the sauce. Put an airtight covering over the bowl and transfer to the fridge. Leave for several hours to mature – preferably overnight.

Ketchup

For the ketchup

Base Roast Tomato Sauce

3–4 red Jalapeño chillies, deseeded and very finely chopped, or to taste

100 ml/scant ½ cup cider vinegar, or to taste

100 g/½ cup muscovado/ molasses sugar, or to taste

1 teaspoon celery seeds

1 teaspoon dried onion powder

1 tablespoon sweet paprika

1 tablespoon freshly ground black pepper

½ teaspoon dried oregano

½ teaspoon ground allspice

½ teaspoon ground coriander

¼ teaspoon ground cumin

¼ teaspoon cayenne pepper

a good pinch of ground mace

a good pinch of ground cinnamon

1 teaspoon sea salt, or to taste

Put the Base Roast Tomato Sauce and the remaining ingredients in a large heavy-based saucepan over medium-low heat and gently heat, stirring constantly, until all the sugar has dissolved. Bring to a simmer and continue to cook over low heat for 45 minutes. Taste and season with more salt, sugar or vinegar as required. At this point I often give the mixture a blitz using a stick blender or food processor to ensure the sauce is velvety smooth.

Return to the heat and continue to cook, stirring regularly, until you have achieved the consistency of ketchup you like. Pour into sterilized bottles or jars and seal with an airtight lid. This ketchup should keep for up to a month in the fridge.

You can easily make the ketchup using canned tomatoes, or preferably passata (Italian sieved tomatoes). Be sure to add some roasted garlic, a little olive oil and perhaps some additional herbs at the ketchup-making stage to give you some added flavour. It is also a great idea to make this with other chillies. This recipe is brilliant with fruity Habaneros substituted for the Jalapeños.

I would use this: as a replacement for your regular ketchup.

Texas-Style Hot Green Chilli Sauce (opposite: top)

Depending on where you live, you may only have come across canned tomatillos in a briny solution, and as such, they bear no relation to the real things at all. They grow well, however, so if you have managed to grow tomatoes, think about planting a few tomatillos alongside them. In Texas they are commonplace and provide the green colour for this sauce – the standard sauce for enchiladas. It's also great with nachos!

500 g/1 lb. 2 oz. tomatillos, roasted under a hot grill/broiler (see page 83)

4 spring onions/scallions, roughly chopped

a small handful of coriander/cilantro, chopped

2–3 garlic cloves, roughly chopped

½ teaspoon sugar

juice from ½ lime

5–6 Serrano chillies, deseeded

1 teaspoon vegetable bouillon powder

½ teaspoon dried mushroom powder

Squeeze the contents of the blackened tomatillos into a food processor or blender. If they are at all tough, discard the skins. Add the remaining ingredients and pulse until all the ingredients are evenly blended.

Pour the mixture into a small saucepan over medium heat and bring gently to a simmer. Cook for 5–10 minutes until softened, and serve.

I would use this: as an alternative salsa for nachos, on enchiladas or on grilled/broiled fish.

New Mexican Green Chilli Sauce (opposite: bottom)

Unlike their neighbours' version in Texas, a New Mex green chilli sauce is very unlikely to contain tomatillos, and the colour comes exclusively from the green chillies used to make the sauce.

2 tablespoons vegetable oil

1 onion, finely chopped

2 garlic cloves, finely chopped

1 tablespoon flour

½ teaspoon ground cumin

300 ml/1¼ cups chicken stock

1 teaspoon dried Mexican oregano

8 green New Mexico chillies, roasted (see page 83), peeled and finely chopped (or, for more heat, use a few Serrano chillies, or Jalapeño and Anaheim)

sea salt and freshly ground black pepper

Heat the oil in a saucepan over medium heat. Add the onion and fry for 2–3 minutes until softened. Add the garlic and fry for a further 1 minute. Stir in the flour and cumin and continue to cook for a further 3 minutes, stirring frequently. Gradually add the stock, stirring constantly, then bring the mixture to a simmer.

Add the oregano and cook for 30 minutes, or until the sauce begins to thicken. Add the chillies, stir well and cook for 5 minutes. Season, then blend using a stick blender, if you like, or serve in a more chunky form. This sauce is always served hot and is generally made fresh every day.

I would use this: as a breakfast sauce for eggs and fried potato, on tacos, or even with chilli nachos.

Hot and Sweet Chilli Dipping Sauce

This is a delightful sauce with strong savoury flavours. If you are feeling adventurous, try adding a tablespoonful of the sauce when making lentil soup, or mixing it with grated cheese before making a cheese and ham toasted sandwich. It is popular with spicy pizza too!

2 tablespoons white wine vinegar

110 g/generous ½ cup sugar

120 g/4¼ oz. ripe red sweet/bell peppers, deseeded and finely chopped

5 cm/2 inches fresh ginger, peeled and grated

1–2 Habanero chillies, deseeded and finely chopped

juice of ½ lime, or to taste

zest of 1 lemon

a good pinch of sea salt

¼ teaspoon fennel seeds

a good pinch of ground coriander

a good pinch of ground cumin

Pour the vinegar and 2 tablespoons water into a medium saucepan. Heat gently, then add the sugar and stir until it has dissolved. Add the red peppers, ginger and chillies. Continue to heat until the mixture comes to a gentle boil, stirring regularly.

Add the remaining ingredients, mix well and continue to cook for 30 minutes, or until the mixture has reduced and thickened. Carefully taste – it will be hot! Season with a little more salt, if required, and perhaps a squeeze more of lime juice. Pour into a sterilized jar, seal and cool. Store in a cool, dark place. Do not refrigerate, as this can cause the sauce to crystallize. Serve at room temperature as a spicy sweet dip.

I would use this: to serve with fish cakes or spring rolls, or as a marinade for salmon steaks.

Chilli Barbecue Baste

Basting involves periodically coating a piece of meat or fish with a sauce, marinade and/or its own juices as it cooks. It is an excellent technique for cooking on a barbecue, and this sauce provides flavour and a subtle heat that builds up over the cooking time. Equally, the butter that is the base of this recipe helps to replace the moisture that evaporates from the meat as it cooks. The end result should be succulent meat with a spicy, caramelized coating — exactly what we want from a barbecue.

125 g/1 stick salted butter

juice of 1 lemon

2 teaspoons muscovado/ molasses sugar

2 garlic cloves, finely chopped

1 teaspoon tomato purée/paste

½ teaspoon dried oregano

1 tablespoon Worcestershire sauce

1 tablespoon hot sauce, such as Trees Can't Dance Flaming Lips Hot Sauce

sea salt and freshly ground black pepper

Gently heat the butter in a medium saucepan over medium heat until it melts. Add the lemon juice and bring to a very gentle simmer, being careful not to burn the butter.

Add the sugar and stir until it dissolves. Add the garlic and tomato purée/paste and gently cook, being careful once again not to burn the butter or the garlic. Add the oregano, Worcestershire sauce and hot sauce. Remove from the heat, season with salt and pepper and use immediately.

I would use this: to baste chicken, pork or veggie dishes while they are cooking, or to coat meat, fish or vegetable kebabs/kabobs before they are barbecued.

Roasted Pepper and Caramelized Onion Burger Relish

Relishes are often categorized as either ketchup-based (for burgers) or mustard-based (for hotdogs). They can be sweet, savoury, spicy, mild, sharp or even sour. In fact the classic American "relishes" actually refer to dill-pickled mini cucumbers/gherkins that were traditionally served as a side to a burger. Relishes originate in India, and were born out of the necessity to preserve fresh fruit and vegetables. This recipe is the root of one of my favourite chilli sauces, but it started life as a relish recipe. Rather than using the conventional tomato base, it uses roasted sweet peppers, whose natural sweetness balances very well with the acidity of the vinegar. The result is sweet, sour and spicy — perfect with slightly smoky burgers. For a hot, smoky relish, reduce the fresh chilli content and add a generous teaspoon of crushed Chipotle chilli. For a delicious North African relish, to serve with lamb burgers, substitute My Favourite Jordanian Baharat Blend (page 82) for the Cajun spice blend and add 3–4 finely chopped sun-dried apricots.

2 ripe Romano-style red sweet/bell peppers

2 tablespoons sunflower oil

1 large onion, diced

2 garlic cloves, crushed

2 tablespoons cider vinegar

1 tablespoon red wine vinegar

2 tablespoons brown sugar

2–3 red Jalapeño chillies (or other red chillies), chopped

1 tablespoon tomato purée/paste

2 teaspoons Cajun spice blend

½ teaspoon paprika (you can use Pimentón Dulce if you want a smoky-flavoured relish)

Put the peppers on a baking sheet and put under a hot grill/broiler. When the skin has blackened on top, turn them over and repeat the process. Once all the skin is charred, turn off the grill/broiler and put the peppers into a medium food bag. Seal the top and set aside to cool. When cool, peel the charred skins away from the flesh and deseed the peppers. Roughly dice the roasted pepper flesh.

Heat the oil in a medium heavy-based saucepan over medium-high heat and fry the onion for 10–15 minutes, or until gradually caramelized. Stir frequently to prevent it from burning. When it has a nice golden colour, add the garlic and fry for 30 seconds–1 minute, or until softened and golden. Add the peppers, both types of vinegar and the sugar. Bring to the boil, stirring constantly to dissolve the sugar (you can add a splash of water if needed). Reduce the heat and stir in the chillies, tomato purée/paste, Cajun spice and paprika. Add 100 ml/scant ½ cup of water and return to a simmer. Cook for 10–15 minutes, stirring regularly and adding a little more water if required, until rich and thick. Adding little and often, and only if really needed, is best, as we want the end relish to be rich, thick and sticky. Pour straight into a sterilized jar and seal. Leave to cool. Store in the fridge once opened.

I would use this: with homemade burgers; it's also perfect with chipotle beef, lamb or chicken, or with veggie dishes.

Noted Chillies: Kashmiri, Pusa Jawala (pictured here, right), Naga Jolokia, Naga Morich (pictured here, left), Lal Mirch (red chilli), Guntur

Chilli Facts and Fiction: In Northern India, dried ground Naga chillies are used to deter marauding wild elephants. The elephant's olfactory sense is so acute that this powdered chilli causes it immediate discomfort if it sniffs even the tiniest amount.

A combination of chillies and lemons are hung above the entrance to a house to deter evil.

Chapter Six

India

India is the world's largest producer of chillies with up to 2.5 million acres used for commercial chilli production. Andhra Pradesh is the state that produces the most chillies. The State's spice capital has to be Guntur. Not only has it a chilli named after it but also the town's agricultural market trades in a single commodity – chillies.

- Goa was the first city in India to trade in chillies. This was the result of the Portuguese taking over the long established spice trade in the region when they conquered Goa in 1510. Chillies soon became an essential part of agriculture and the diet of the region, and by 1542 chillies were so well established that at least 3 were classified as being Indian. Soon chillies were being sold along with the other spices and formed the foundation of a trade that still thrives today.

- Most of India's chillies are part of the genus *Capsicum Annuum* and are very closely related to the Cayenne and New Mexico varieties of chilli. The majority of red chillies are used in their dried form, although green chillies are used fresh. Kashmiri chillies are the most commonly used in India. They are not particularly hot and are used dried to impart a distinct flavour and rich red colour to dishes. It is also worth noting that they do not come from Kashmir!

- The infamous ultra-hot Naga chillies also originate from Assam in North East India. They are among the very few *Capsicum Chinense* species grown in India.

Vindaloo Curry Paste

A vindaloo is still something of a maligned curry – a joke dish that is too hot to be enjoyed and only eaten by the foolish and/or drunk. The reality, however, is very different. It is one of the most finely flavoured curries you can make and, although often very hot, it is rarely uncomfortably so. This paste is my absolute favourite of the many (many) I have made, and it works equally well with pork, lamb or even beef. I would definitely recommend making it at least 24 hours in advance of using it, to get the best flavour. I have kept it in a sealed pot in my fridge for weeks, and it only improves over time. My top tips are: take a few spoonfuls to marinate the meat for a few hours before actually cooking the curry; use more onions than you think you need (ensuring you get some colour into them by frying before adding the other ingredients); and slow cook it, if you have time – 24 hours at around 80°C (175°F) is about perfect.

1 teaspoon cumin seeds

5 cloves

5-cm/2-inch piece cinnamon
   stick, roughly broken

8 black peppercorns

1 green cardamom pod

¼ piece star anise

1 teaspoon black onion seeds

3-cm/1¼-inch piece fresh
   ginger, peeled and roughly
   chopped

6 large garlic cloves, peeled

1 tablespoon unsweetened
   tamarind paste

5 teaspoons cider vinegar

4 tablespoons plus 1 teaspoon
   vegetable oil

10–20 chillies, deseeded, such
   as a mixture of green Finger
   chillies and red Bird's Eyes,
   to taste

Put the cumin seeds in a heavy-based pan over medium heat and add the cloves, cinnamon, peppercorns, cardamom and star anise. Lightly toast the spices, shaking the pan frequently. Allow to cool slightly. Remove the seeds from the cardamom pod and put into a spice grinder. Add the other roasted ingredients and the onion seeds, and grind into a coarse powder. (Alternatively, use a pestle and mortar.)

Put the ginger and garlic into a mini food processor and add the tamarind, vinegar, oil and chillies. Tip in the ground spices and blitz into a smooth paste. Pack the mixture into a container and seal tightly. Put into the fridge and allow to mature for at least 24 hours before using.

I would use this: to marinate pork, lamb, beef or vegetables before cooking. See also page 105.

Sambar Powder

Full of delicious southern Indian flavours, this powder can be added to any dish. It's great in soups or for flavouring vegetarian dishes.

10 dried red chillies

4 tablespoons coriander seeds

2 tablespoons cumin seeds

2 teaspoons fenugreek seeds

2 teaspoons black peppercorns

1 teaspoon black onion seeds

2 teaspoons toovar dal (pigeon peas)

2 teaspoons chana dal (yellow split peas)

2 teaspoons urad dal (split black gram)

20 dried curry leaves

2 teaspoons ground turmeric

1 teaspoon ground asafoetida

Put the chillies in heavy-based saucepan over medium heat and add the coriander, cumin, fenugreek seeds, peppercorns and onion seeds. Toast the spices until they begin to release their aromas, shaking the pan frequently.

Tip the spices into a bowl and repeat the same process with the dals, being careful not let them burn. Tip them into the bowl with the spices, then transfer them all to a spice grinder or mortar, add the curry leaves and grind to a fairly fine powder. Stir in the turmeric and asafoetida. Transfer to an airtight container and store in cool dark place until you are ready to use it.

I would use this: to flavour lentils or to thicken a spicy sauce.

Lamb Vindaloo

This is not a quick dish to make. Ideally, the paste is made at least 48 hours ahead and the meat is marinated for a further 24. The cooking requires little attention at the start, but it needs time to cook to perfection – the slower you cook this the better it is. These naans are the perfect accompaniment.

For the curry

700 g/1 lb. 9 oz. lamb, cubed

Vindaloo Curry Paste (page 102)

1–2 tablespoons nut oil or sunflower oil

3 large onions, 2 thinly sliced; 1 chopped

400 ml/1¾ cups chicken or vegetable stock

400-g/14-oz. can chopped tomatoes

15–20 curry leaves

1 teaspoon palm sugar

1 teaspoon sea salt, or to taste

Serves 4

Curry

Put the lamb in a large bowl and add 1–2 tablespoons of the Vindaloo Curry Paste. Mix together thoroughly. Cover and marinate in the fridge for 3 hours or preferably overnight.

Heat the oil in a large heavy-based saucepan over medium-high heat and add the onions. Cook for 15–20 minutes until they are well coloured and softened. Add the remaining Vindaloo Curry Paste and stir well to combine with the onions. Fry for a further 5 minutes, or until you can see the paste has started to cook through. If the paste looks like it is sticking too much in the pan (a little is actually quite desirable), add a little water as required, a tablespoon at a time.

Move the onions to one side and add the marinated lamb to the pan. Brown the lamb on all sides to seal in the juices. Add the stock and tomatoes and bring back to the boil, stirring frequently. Add the curry leaves and sugar and season to taste with the salt – it may need a little more than 1 teaspoon.

Cover and cook in a low oven – 100°C (200°F) Gas ½ – for as long as you can (we cooked it for 24 hours at about 80°C (175°F) and it was indescribably wonderful), or in a slow cooker. Or cook it on the hob/stovetop over very low heat for 2–3 hours.

Naan breads

For the naan breads

250 g/2 cups strong white bread flour, plus extra to dust

250 g/2 cups plain/all-purpose flour

10 g/2 teaspoons sea salt

5 g/⅛ oz. fast-action dried yeast

160 ml/⅔ cup warm water

160 ml/⅔ cup plain/natural yogurt, warmed

1 tablespoon olive oil, plus extra to grease

ghee, oil or butter, to serve

Put all the dry ingredients in a large bowl. Add the water, yogurt and oil and, using your hands, knead the ingredients together for 10 minutes, or until you have a stretchy, slightly sticky dough. Flour the work surface. Divide the dough into small-lemon-sized portions. Make each into a ball and roll out to make thin 20-cm/8-inch rounds. Make sure each side is floured to prevent sticking and stack them on a plate. Cover with foil and allow to rise in a warm place for 10 minutes.

Heat a heavy-based frying pan over high heat and lightly grease it. Cook the naans for 2 minutes, or until they rise and begin to blister. Flip them over and repeat. Rub with ghee, oil or butter and stack in a warm oven until you are ready to eat. Serve with the curry.

Sri Lankan Dark Roast Curry Paste

The flavour and appearance of this paste rely on the spices being well toasted, but if any are burnt they will ruin the final result. With this in mind, I tend to toast the coriander, cinnamon and cloves together, and then repeat the process with the cumin, fennel and fenugreek, adding the cardamom seeds (minus the pod!) for the last 30 seconds or so of toasting. Make sure each is beginning to colour but that none have been singed on the pan. To do this, it is ideal to keep the seeds moving as they toast.

5 tablespoons coriander seeds

5-cm/2-inch stick cinnamon, broken into pieces

½ teaspoon cloves

4 teaspoons cumin seeds

2 teaspoons fennel seeds

1 teaspoon fenugreek seeds

½ teaspoon cardamom seeds

8 large dried red chillies, deseeded

1 tablespoon nut oil

2 large garlic cloves

2.5-cm/1-inch piece fresh ginger, peeled and chopped

2-cm/¾-inch piece lemongrass, tough outer leaves removed, chopped

2 tablespoons coconut milk

2 tablespoons cider vinegar

1 tablespoon lime juice

Put the coriander, cinnamon and cloves in a heavy-based saucepan and toast over medium heat until they begin to darken and release their aromas, shaking the pan frequently. Remove from the pan and toast the remaining spice seeds in the same way. Allow to cool and grind to a fine powder using a grinder or pestle and mortar.

Put all the spices in a food processor or blender with the chillies and oil. Blend together, adding the garlic, ginger and lemongrass, and gradually adding the coconut milk, vinegar and lime juice to make a smooth, fragrant paste. Loosen with a little water if required. Blend until you have a smooth and glossy paste.

Store in an airtight container in the fridge. It will happily keep for several weeks like this.

I would use this: to make a delicious prawn/shrimp curry.

Sour Fish Curry Paste

I often make this particular paste and love the buttery-ness the fenugreek imparts to the final curry, perfect with the sourness of the kokum or tamarind. The little hint of aniseed that fennel seeds give is virtually indispensable in fish curries and the addition of thin slices of fresh fennel bulb to a lighter curry is something that is hard to beat. This also works very well with chicken – as does the fresh fennel!

1 teaspoon fenugreek seeds

1 teaspoon mustard seeds

½ teaspoon fennel seeds

8–10 red chillies, deseeded and chopped

1 teaspoon sea salt

2 pieces kokum, soaked in warm water to soften (or 1 teaspoon unsweetened tamarind paste)

6 garlic cloves, peeled and chopped

10 curry leaves

1 shallot, chopped

3 tablespoons vegetable oil

1 teaspoon ground turmeric

Put the fenugreek, mustard and fennel seeds in a saucepan and toast until the mustard seeds start to pop. Set aside to cool, then grind to a fine powder using a grinder or a pestle and mortar.

Put the chillies, salt, kokum, garlic, curry leaves and shallot into a blender, then process, adding the vegetable oil while mixing. Add the ground toasted spices and the turmeric, and give everything a final blitz to ensure an even mix.

I would use this: to make the perfect fish curry; ideal with monkfish.

Xacuti Curry Powder

This powder recipe can also be made using fresh ingredients as a paste. It originates from Goa and, as such, is strongly associated with the fine seafood curries of that coastline. This recipe works particularly well with crab, fish or prawns/shrimp, although it can easily be used with chicken or to create a delicious vegetarian curry. It has a distinct hint of aniseed from the star anise and the fennel seeds, which balance beautifully with the sweetness of the coconut and the warmth of the chillies, peppercorns and ginger.

120 g/1⅓ cups desiccated/ unsweetened shredded coconut (or flesh from ½ fresh coconut, grated)

6–8 red Kashmiri chillies, deseeded

6 cloves

1 star anise

5-cm/2-inch piece cinnamon stick, broken up

1 teaspoon black peppercorns

1 teaspoon cumin seeds

1 tablespoon coriander seeds

¼ teaspoon fenugreek seeds

1 teaspoon fennel seeds

1 tablespoon poppy seeds

4–5 dried garlic flakes

1 teaspoon ground turmeric

½ teaspoon grated nutmeg

¼ teaspoon ground ginger

Heat a heavy-based frying pan over medium heat. If you are using fresh coconut, toast this in the pan first until it just begins to colour around the edges. Brush out into a bowl and set aside. Return the pan to the heat and add the chillies, cloves, star anise, cinnamon, peppercorns, cumin, coriander, fenugreek and fennel seeds. Toast for a few minutes until they begin to release their aromas. Add the poppy seeds (and desiccated coconut, if you are using this) and toast for a further 1–2 minutes. Allow to cool then put into a spice grinder along with the fresh coconut, if using, and the dried garlic. Blitz to a fine powder and then stir in the turmeric, nutmeg and ginger.

To make this as a paste: replace the matching dry ingredients with the following fresh ones: fresh coconut, 4–5 garlic cloves and a 2.5-cm/ 1-inch piece of fresh ginger. When blending, add 1 tablespoon of vegetable oil to the mix and add water as required to achieve your preferred paste consistency.

I would use this: with a little water to make a paste and add to frying onions to create the flavouring sauce for a great seafood curry.

Nepalese Sekuwa Marinade

Marinating in yogurt is traditional throughout the Middle East and Asia. In fact, the word "yogurt" is a Turkish word. The process of fermenting the milk turns the yogurt acidic and so it acts to tenderize meat in the same way that a vinegar- or citrus-based marinade would. There are virtually limitless ways of flavouring this base and, because the resulting marinades coat the meat so well, they tend to produce really juicy and flavoursome results. This is perfect for meat skewers – they should be grilled/broiled or barbecued once they have been marinated.

1 tablespoon cumin seeds

1 teaspoon coriander seeds

1 teaspoon black peppercorns

¼ teaspoon Szechuan pepper

1 teaspoon sea salt, or to taste

½ teaspoon ground turmeric

1 large onion, finely chopped

2–3 celery sticks, chopped

3 red Bird's Eye chillies

2 garlic cloves

2-cm/¾-inch piece fresh ginger, peeled and sliced

juice of ½ lemon

2 tablespoons mustard oil

1 tablespoon soy sauce

500 ml/2 cups plain/natural yogurt

a small bunch of coriander/cilantro or dill, chopped

Put the cumin and coriander seeds in a heavy-based saucepan over medium heat and lightly toast, shaking the pan frequently. Tip into a mortar or spice grinder and add the peppercorns, Szechuan pepper and salt. Grind well, then stir in the turmeric.

Put all the spices into a food processor or blender with the onion, celery, chillies, garlic and ginger. Pulse a few times to roughly blend. Add the lemon juice, oil and soy sauce, and blend into a smooth paste. Tip into a bowl and stir in the yogurt and coriander/cilantro.

I would use this: for chicken or lamb skewers.

Bengali Kasundi (Mustard and Chilli Relish)

There are many ways to prepare the Indian relish, Kasundi, but it always contains mustard seeds – usually soaked in vinegar – and chillies. The first of the variations here was supplied to me by the incredible Simon Majumdar. I needed to define the classic Kasundi, so I immediately thought of him. Simon's legendary travels in search of ever more things to eat and write about make him almost unbearably knowledgeable about a truly vast range of exotic world cuisines. And, as I always say, if you can't rely on a Welsh Bengali Englishman from Yorkshire living in LA for authenticity, then Lord help us all.

Simon's Kasundi (opposite: top)

100 g/⅓ cup yellow mustard seeds

100 ml/scant ½ cup palm vinegar

4 green Finger chillies, deseeded and finely chopped

4 large garlic cloves, finely chopped

5-cm/2-inch piece fresh ginger, peeled and chopped

1 teaspoon sugar

a good squeeze of lime juice

vegetable oil, as needed (optional)

zest of ½ lime

Put the mustard seeds in a heavy-based saucepan over medium heat and toast until they begin to pop, shaking the pan frequently to avoid scorching any of the seeds. Remove from the pan and set aside to cool. Soak the mustard seeds in the palm vinegar, preferably overnight, then drain and reserve the vinegar.

Put the mustard seeds in a food processor or blender with the chillies, garlic, ginger, sugar and lime juice. Blend until you have a smooth paste. Add a little of the reserved vinegar, or some oil or water, if required, to aid blending. (Using water or oil will impact on the amount of time the finished product can be kept, so if you plan to make a larger batch and store it, use vinegar.) Add the lime zest and stir thoroughly. Transfer to a sterilized jar with an airtight lid and store in the fridge until required. It will keep for about 2 weeks.

Variation 1 (opposite: bottom right)
Another "raw" Kasundi with the added fruitiness of green mango.

2 tablespoons yellow mustard seeds, soaked for 24 hours in cider vinegar

5 small hot red chillies, deseeded and roughly chopped

3 garlic cloves, crushed

1 small green mango, peeled and roughly chopped

1 teaspoon sugar

sea salt

Put all the ingredients into a food processor or blender and process until you have a smooth paste. Season as required with salt. Transfer to an airtight container and store in the fridge until required.

Variation 2 (above: bottom left)
A "cooked" Kasundi that incorporates fresh tomatoes. Pour into a jar when hot for the best keeping properties.

4 tablespoons vegetable oil

1 tablespoon yellow mustard seeds

1 tablespoon black mustard seeds

1 teaspoon cumin seeds

1 teaspoon coriander seeds

4 garlic cloves

5-cm/2-inch piece fresh ginger

4 hot green Finger chillies, finely chopped

100 ml/scant ½ cup cider vinegar

1 teaspoon ground turmeric

4 large ripe tomatoes

2 teaspoons sugar

2 teaspoons sea salt

Heat the oil in a heavy-based saucepan over medium heat. Add both types of mustard seed, the cumin and coriander and gently fry for about 4–5 minutes stirring constantly. Add the garlic, ginger, chillies and vinegar, and cook for another 4–5 minutes. Stir in the turmeric, tomatoes, sugar and salt. Bring to a simmer and cook for a further 10–15 minutes until the contents of the pan have reduced and thickened. With a stick blender or in a food processor blend the contents of the pan into a smooth paste. Transfer to a sterilized container while still hot, seal and store in the fridge.

I would use any of these: in sandwiches, with your favourite curry, or with spicy beef dishes.

Pyaj Ko Achar (Nepalese Onion Chutney) (below: left)

Achars are fresh chutneys. They are easy to make, taste delicious and look attractive at the table. They come in an unending array of styles and use an equally extensive range of cooking and preparation methods. This one has a great combination of flavours and a quite unexpected "crunch" from the deep-fried mustard seeds.

2 tablespoons vegetable oil

2 red onions, peeled and chopped

6 garlic cloves, peeled and roughly chopped

2 tablespoons chana dal

2 hot red chillies, stalks removed, chopped

1 teaspoon tamarind paste (or a good squeeze of lemon juice)

1 tablespoon yellow mustard seeds

a pinch of fenugreek seeds

a pinch of dried thyme

2 fresh curry leaves, torn

sea salt

Heat 1 tablespoon of the oil in a heavy-based saucepan over medium heat and fry the onions, garlic, dal and chillies until the onions have taken on a golden colour. Remove from the heat and spoon into a mortar, then add the tamarind paste and a good seasoning of salt. Pound this mixture using a pestle. This process will take some time! Once this is smooth, scrape it out into a serving bowl.

Wipe out the pan and heat the remaining oil over medium heat. Add the mustard seeds and fenugreek and cook until the mustard seeds start to pop. Add the thyme and curry leaves, and cook for 15 seconds. Pour this oil over the other ingredients in the serving bowl.

I would use this: as a dip for homemade roti or flatbreads, or raw vegetables.

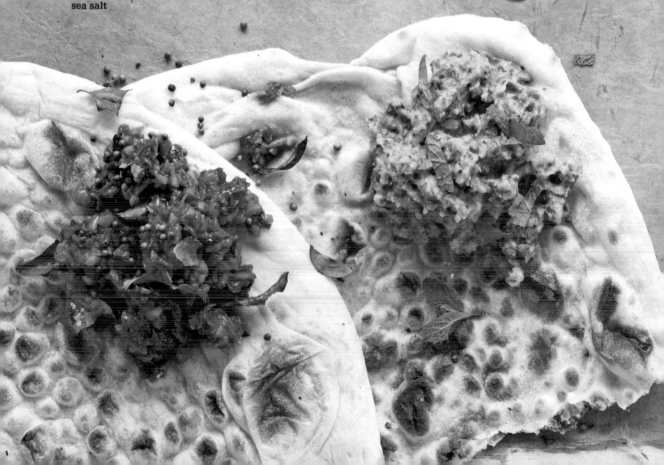

Sabse Borani

Although originally designed to be served as sour yogurt drinks, Sabse recipes make delicious dips, and this recipe from Afghanistan is no exception. There is a gentle sweetness from the caramelized onions and a warming zing from the dried chilli powder. Reduce the chilli powder if serving with a hot curry.

250 g/1 cup plain/natural
  yogurt

a large handful of spinach

2 tablespoons vegetable oil

1 onion, finely chopped

2 garlic cloves, very finely
  chopped

1 teaspoon hot chilli powder
  (Naga powder, if you dare)

a squeeze of lemon juice

sea salt and freshly ground
  black pepper

2–3 mint leaves, to garnish

Put the yogurt in muslin/cheesecloth and suspend over a bowl. Leave for 1 hour or until any excess moisture has drained away, squeezing the muslin occasionally. Heat a saucepan over medium heat. Add 2 tablespoons water and the spinach leaves. Reduce the heat, cover and allow the spinach to wilt, then remove from the heat, drain and set aside.

Heat the oil in a frying pan over medium heat. Add the onion and fry, stirring constantly, until it is evenly golden brown but not burnt. Add a little water to the pan if required. Add the garlic and chilli powder and fry for a further 2 minutes. Stir in the spinach and cook for a further minute. Remove from the heat and allow to cool to room temperature.

Put the onion and spinach mixture in a small bowl and add the yogurt. Stir well until they are thoroughly mixed. Season to taste with salt and pepper. Squeeze the lemon juice over the dip and garnish with fresh mint leaves. Serve at room temperature.

I would use this: mixed with spiced grilled/broiled fish in a flatbread.

Babari Ko Achar (Mint and Chilli Chutney) (opposite: right)

A fresh, fiery, minty dip from Nepal/Northern India, Babari Ko Achar is an ideal complement to the onion chutney opposite. Great with flatbreads or with spicy marinated meat kebabs/kabobs.

a large handful of mint, roughly
  chopped

2 green chillies, such as
  Jalapeños, deseeded and
  roughly chopped

1 red onion, roughly chopped

3 garlic cloves, roughly
  chopped

2.5-cm/1-inch piece fresh
  ginger, peeled and finely
  chopped

125 g/½ cup plain/natural
  yogurt

juice of 1 lemon

sea salt

Put the mint, chillies, onion, garlic and ginger into a food processor or blender and pulse together. Add the yogurt and continue to blend into a smooth paste. Scrape down the sides of the blender as required, to ensure an even mix. Add the lemon juice and pulse to combine. Season with salt to taste. Transfer to a bowl and serve. If covered, it can be stored in the fridge for a few days until required, but always bring it to room temperature before serving.

I would use this: to serve with tandoori trout, rotis and fresh, crunchy salad.

Jalfrezi Paste

A dish that originated in China but is now a Bengali classic, the jalfrezi is a strongly flavoured, dry curry. This version is the paste that I have finally, through trial and error, found gives a lovely blend of flavour, heat and colour. As is traditional with a jalfrezi, I still like to add a few sliced fresh green chillies to the final curry towards the end of cooking, making the final dish not only delicious but pretty fiery too. It is good to know, also, that these drier Indian curries are often a much healthier option to choose when eating out, as they tend not to be cooked in ghee (clarified butter) and do not compromise at all on flavour.

2 teaspoons white cumin seeds

1 teaspoon pink peppercorns

1 teaspoon mustard seeds

1 teaspoon fenugreek seeds

1 teaspoon coriander seeds

1 cardamom pod

2 cloves

2 large garlic cloves, peeled

5-cm/2-inch piece fresh ginger, peeled and roughly chopped

½ teaspoon sea salt

juice of ½ lemon

2 tablespoons groundnut oil

2 tablespoons tomato purée/paste

1 teaspoon ground turmeric

2 Bird's Eye chillies, deseeded and chopped

1 hot green chilli, deseeded and chopped

a small bunch of coriander/cilantro, finely chopped

Put the cumin seeds in a heavy-based saucepan over medium heat and add the peppercorns, mustard seeds, fenugreek seeds, coriander seeds, cardamom and cloves. Toast gently until the mustard seeds start to pop, shaking the pan frequently to prevent scorching. Allow to cool slightly, then remove the cardamom seeds from the pod and discard the husk. Grind these toasted spices and the cardamom seeds with a mortar and pestle or spice grinder until you have a fairly fine powder.

Put the ground spices into a mini food processor or mortar and add the garlic, ginger and salt, then blitz or pound to break them down. Add the lemon juice, oil and tomato purée/paste and pound/blitz to a smooth paste. Add the turmeric and both types of chillies and continue to pound/blitz until smooth. Finally, add the coriander/cilantro and mix well.

Pack into an airtight container and store in the fridge until you are ready to use it.

I would use this: to cook with chicken, prawns/shrimp or vegetables. See also page 116.

Kashmiri Lamb Marinade

Kashmiri chillies are slightly less pungent than the majority of chillies found in north Indian food. They are bred to have a very fine distinctive flavour and to add vibrant colour to any dish. The beauty of their slightly less intense heat is that you can add a significant number to virtually any dish, getting all the benefits of their great flavour and colour without making the resulting dish unpleasantly hot. For this dish, it is necessary to prepare them and make them into a powder. To do this, it is best to lightly toast the fresh chillies in a cast iron pan or griddle until they begin to release their aroma and the skins start to darken. Deseed the chillies and finely chop them. Pound to a coarse powder or flakes using a mortar and pestle or a spice grinder. The powder or flakes can be stored in an airtight jar in a cool, dark place until required.

2 teaspoons Kashmiri chilli powder (or flakes)

¼ teaspoon ground cardamom

1 teaspoon garam masala

1 teaspoon sea salt flakes, or to taste

120 g/½ cup full-fat plain/natural yogurt

2.5-cm/1-inch piece fresh ginger, peeled and very finely chopped

2 garlic cloves, peeled and crushed

a small handful of coriander/cilantro leaves and stalks, finely chopped

a squeeze of lemon juice

Put the chilli powder in a medium bowl and add the other dry spices and the salt. Pour in the yogurt and stir well. Add the ginger, garlic and coriander/cilantro, and mix together thoroughly. Add a little more salt to taste, if required, and a good squeeze of lemon juice. Cover and leave in the fridge for 1 hour for the flavours to mingle.

I would use this: to marinate lamb or chicken.

Jalfrezi Curry

Despite my recent leanings towards vindaloo, at heart I love jalfrezi the most of all curries. You can't beat the fresh green chillies. This recipe uses the great flavour of chicken thighs, which are always preferable to breast meat. Try to buy organic, but always buy free-range. Compared to the cost it would be if the retail price for a chicken had risen in line with inflation since the early 1970s (several times what we pay today), buying the better-quality organic free-range doesn't seem excessive at all. An absolutely delicious alternative to this is to use pheasant. It is comparatively cheap, always free-range and low in fat.

This is anything but a traditional recipe. I have incorporated potatoes and mushrooms, which work very well with the chicken and are winners in most dishes. I have also included broccoli stalks – a delicious ingredient, which is often inexplicably thrown away. They add lots of flavour and goodness. An all-round fine ingredient!

1 tablespoon vegetable oil

500 g/1 lb. 2 oz. skinlesss, boneless free-range chicken thighs, cut into 4-cm/ 1½-inch cubes

1 large onion, chopped

2–3 tablespoons Jalfrezi Paste (page 114)

4 small waxy potatoes, cut into 2.5-cm/1-inch cubes

2 large Portobello mushrooms, roughly chopped

1 Romano-style (sweet pointed) red sweet/bell pepper, deseeded and finely chopped

stalks from 2 broccoli heads, finely chopped

about 500 ml/2 cups hot chicken stock

3–4 Indian Finger chillies, cut diagonally into 5-mm/¼-inch slices

sea salt and freshly ground black pepper

coriander/cilantro leaves, roughly chopped

cooked basmati rice, to serve

Heat the oil in a large heavy-based saucepan over medium heat and fry the chicken meat all over to seal it. Remove from the pan and set aside. Add the onion to the pan and cook it for 5–10 minutes until it begins to soften and develop some colour. Add the Jalfrezi Paste and continue to cook, stirring constantly. Reduce the heat and cook for 5 minutes, then increase the heat and return the chicken to the pan.

Add the potatoes, mushrooms, sweet/bell pepper and broccoli, and stir well. Cook for 3 minutes, then add 3 ladlefuls of the chicken stock. Return to the boil and reduce to a simmer. Add the sliced chillies and continue to cook at a gentle simmer for 30 minutes, or until the chicken and potatoes are cooked through. Keep adding a ladleful of the stock as required during cooking. Jalfrezi is best served as quite a dry curry, so it is better to be frugal with the stock rather than generous. Season as required with salt and pepper. Garnish with coriander/cilantro and serve with cooked basmati rice.

This recipe also works very well as a vegetarian dish. My favourite combination would be cauliflower, potato and mushroom. Cook the onion and the paste as above, then add the potatoes and mushrooms. Add the cauliflower at the same time as the vegetable stock, and cook until the potatoes are just soft.

Noted Chillies: Thai Dragon (pictured here), Bird's Eye, Chi-Chen, Cayenne, Goat's Horn, Japone, Tears of Fire.

Chilli Facts and Fiction: In a recent field test, identical chilli seeds were planted in Indonesia, China, India and Thailand. The fruit from the Indonesian plants were consistently the hottest although, interestingly, in a consumer survey conducted at the same time "pungency" was not the main consideration for Indonesians in general. Perhaps, though, this was because it didn't *need* to be a consideration!

Chapter Seven

South-East Asia

The people of the Caribbean, Mexico and India are all seen as living for chillies, but even they do not consume red-hot dishes with the same enthusiasm as the population of South-East Asia. The food of this region is fragrant and varied in a way that is not really seen anywhere else in the world, and although Mexican and Indian food is full of chillies, the dishes do not consistently have the same range of flavours or intensity of heat as classic Thai or Indonesian dishes.

- Such is the importance of chillies in the diet of Indonesia that when their price on the open market began to reach unprecedented levels and it looked as if they would soon be beyond the means of the general population, the government encouraged every household to grow its own supply of chillies. The possibility that chillies would not be readily available to everyone was something they could not allow to happen.

- A lot of the classic dishes of this area, and particularly from Thailand, revolve around handmade chilli pastes, so to make authentic dishes, a good-quality, heavy pestle and mortar is essential.

- Most chillies used in South-East Asian food come from the *Capsicum Annuum* family. The super-fiery Bird's Eye chilli is perhaps the most commonly used – generally in its green form, and always fresh. There is a delicate floral aftertaste to the Asian Bird's Eye, which is not as apparent in its African relative, and this tends to be lost when the chilli is dried. Other chillies regularly used are the Thai long red, the Banana chilli and the wonderful Thai Dragon.

Thai Green Curry Paste

The key to a good Thai curry of any description is the paste. These pastes are best made using a large and heavy pestle and mortar because it makes the task of pounding the ingredients much easier. By pounding each ingredient to a pulp, you get a smoother and more homogenized paste – the individual ingredients are actually transformed into a single entity. If you use a food processor, no matter how good it is, it is simply cutting the ingredients into smaller and smaller pieces. This does little to actually combine them and leads to a more "bitty" and granular paste. Also, because of the way Thai pastes are subsequently cooked in coconut milk rather than fried in oil they have less opportunity to soften and blend during the cooking process. The traditional process prepares them perfectly for how they are intended to be cooked.

3–4 lemongrass stalks, tough outer leaves discarded, chopped

2-cm/¾-inch piece fresh red turmeric, chopped

10 medium-hot green Thai chillies, deseeded and finely chopped

10 hot green chillies, such as Bird's Eye, deseeded and chopped

2 red shallots, finely sliced

4–5 large garlic cloves, chopped

5–6 frozen kaffir lime leaves (or dried), finely chopped

5-cm/2-inch piece fresh galangal root, peeled and chopped

2-cm/¾-inch piece fresh coriander/cilantro root, chopped

1 teaspoon Thai shrimp paste (gapi)

sea salt and white pepper

Starting with the lemongrass, work through the ingredients list in order. Using a mortar and pestle, pound each ingredient to a smooth paste before adding the next. It is time-consuming and hard work, but the end result is significantly better than a paste made using a food processor. If stored in an airtight container, this paste will keep for up to 4 weeks in the fridge, although it is better made fresh as required.

I would use this: to make the perfect chicken or seafood green curry.

Thai Red Curry Paste

A good Thai red curry paste requires patience and commitment to make well. This is obviously great to make curries with, but I would also recommend it as the key flavouring ingredient for Thai fish cakes. It adds a citrusy little kick and the shrimp paste helps to enhance the flavour of the fish. The other essential ingredient would be finely chopped steamed green beans — well worth trying.

1 teaspoon white peppercorns

2 teaspoons coriander seeds

1 teaspoon cumin seeds

4 cloves

½ teaspoon grated nutmeg

2 small lemongrass stalks, tough outer leaves discarded, chopped

10 red chillies, deseeded and chopped

2 teaspoons kaffir lime zest (available frozen) (or zest of 1 small lime)

2 red shallots, chopped

5–6 garlic cloves, finely chopped

a small handful of coriander/ cilantro leaves and stalks, chopped

½ teaspoon shrimp paste (gapi)

¼ teaspoon sea salt

Put the peppercorns in a saucepan over medium heat and add the coriander seeds, cumin seeds and cloves. Toast until they release their aromas, shaking the pan frequently. Remove from the heat and allow to cool. Using a pestle and mortar, grind the spices to a fine powder. Pour into a small bowl, stir in the nutmeg and set aside.

Take each fresh ingredient in turn and pound it in the mortar into a smooth paste. Ensure that each ingredient is fully broken down before adding the next. Once you have achieved a smooth consistency, scrape the mixture into a small bowl and mix in the finely ground dry spices. Store in an airtight container in the fridge.

I would use this: to cook with chicken, duck, tofu or vegetables, or to flavour Thai fish cakes.

Mussaman Curry Paste

This is perhaps the most famous of all the Thai curry pastes. To make a good mussaman, what seems like an industrial quantity of paste is required. With this in mind it is easier to measure the ingredients by the tablespoon rather than by specifying a number of garlic cloves or lemongrass stalks. The curry originated in Persia but was quickly absorbed into Thai cuisine where it now holds an almost legendary significance. It has become increasingly elaborate over the last few centuries. Thai food specialist, David Thompson, describes the Thai mussaman curry as being "oily, and highly seasoned with tamarind and sugar".

10 long red dried Thai chillies, deseeded

4 tablespoons finely chopped red shallots

4 tablespoons finely chopped garlic cloves

2 tablespoons finely chopped fresh galangal

1 tablespoon finely chopped fresh ginger

2 tablespoons finely chopped fresh lemongrass (tough outer leaves removed)

2 teaspoons finely chopped coriander/cilantro root

1 teaspoon cumin seeds

1 tablespoon coriander seeds

4 cloves

5 black peppercorns

3 cardamom pods

2 small pieces of mace

a small piece of cassia bark (optional)

½ teaspoon sea salt

1 tablespoon salted roasted peanuts

1 teaspoon palm sugar

a little vegetable oil, if needed

Soak the chillies in hot water for 30 minutes. Drain them and squeeze out any excess moisture. Roughly chop the chillies, then put them into a saucepan over low heat and add the shallots, garlic, galangal, ginger, lemongrass and coriander/cilantro root. Roast for a few moments (adding a little water, if required) until they begin to brown and become aromatic. Put these ingredients into a mortar and use a pestle to pound them into a smooth paste.

Put the cumin seeds, coriander seeds, cloves, peppercorns, cardamom, mace and cassia bark (if using) in a frying pan. Toast for a few minutes until they become fragrant, shaking the pan frequently. Allow to cool slightly, then remove the seeds from the cardamom pods and discard the husk. Put the toasted seeds into a clean mortar or a spice grinder and grind to a fine powder.

Add the salt to the lemongrass mixture and continue to pound in the mortar, then add the peanuts and pound further. Sift in the ground dry spices to remove any larger pieces. Add the sugar and continue to pound until you have a smooth, rich paste. Add a little vegetable oil, if necessary, in order to loosen the mixture.

Cover and set aside until you are ready to cook.

I would use this: to make a chicken or beef curry. See also page 124.

Mussaman Curry

I enjoy making a mussaman curry enormously. Rather like the vindaloo curry, it is one for the patient cook who doesn't mind a multi-staged process. My favourite version of this is made with pheasant, but you can just as easily make it with chicken. Certain elements of this curry are also unique: the deep-frying of the potatoes and shallots is not something I would do for any other curry, but it does add to the richness and depth of flavour. It is also key to understand Thai seasoning when cooking a mussaman. To create the perfect flavour you need to balance the saltiness of the fish sauce with the sweetness of the palm sugar and the sourness of the tamarind. The combination of these flavours provides the seasoning for the curry. As with all cooking, though, remember to taste constantly, not only to make sure you are seasoning correctly but also, even more importantly, to see how these seasonings are combining with the other ingredients and how the flavours are developing as you cook. Always remember too, that if you think it tastes great, it probably does!

vegetable oil, for deep-frying

8 skinless, boneless chicken thighs (or duck thighs), each cut into 3 or 4 pieces

6–8 small waxy potatoes, quartered and soaked in cold water for 15 minutes to remove the starch

8 small red shallots, peeled but left whole

3 black cardamom pods

600 ml/2½ cups coconut milk

75 g/½ cup roasted peanuts

4 fresh bay leaves

400 ml/1¾ cups coconut cream

Mussaman Curry Paste (page 123)

50 g/1¾ oz. palm sugar

2 tablespoons Thai fish sauce

2 tablespoons tamarind paste

220 ml/scant 1 cup pineapple juice

jasmine rice and fruit, to serve

Serves 4

Heat the oil for deep-frying in a wok or large heavy-based saucepan to 180°C (350°F) – test by frying a small cube of bread; it should brown in 40 seconds. Deep-fry the meat until golden brown. It won't be cooked through. Remove from the pan and drain on kitchen paper/paper towels. Drain and pat the potatoes dry on kitchen paper/paper towels, then fry with the shallots in the hot oil until cooked and golden.

Put the cardamom pods in a saucepan and lightly toast over medium heat. Remove from the pan and set aside. Put the chicken in the saucepan over medium heat and add the coconut milk. Bring to the boil and add the cardamom pods, peanuts and bay leaves. Cook for 10–15 minutes, or until the chicken is just cooked through, then add the fried potatoes and shallots. Remove from the heat.

In another pan, heat the coconut cream over medium heat until it begins to separate and you can see the coconut oil. Add the Mussaman Curry Paste, then reduce the heat and simmer for 10 minutes, stirring constantly, or until the paste is cooked through and the aroma of the spices is released. Do not allow this to burn! Add half the palm sugar to the pan and continue to cook, stirring regularly, until the sugars begin to caramelize and deepen in colour. Add half the fish sauce and tamarind.

Add the chicken mixture to the pan. Pour in the pineapple juice and stir well. Gently heat through and adjust the seasoning, adding sugar, fish sauce and tamarind to taste – it should taste a beautiful balance of sweet, salty and sour. Serve with rice and fruit.

Nam Prik Pao (below: left)

Whether this is actually a cooking paste, a condiment, a dip or even a jam is a matter of conjecture, but it clearly illustrates the flexibility of the flavours and the many uses to which Nam Prik Pao lends itself. It is delicious with rice, noodles, vegetables, fish and meat. It often finds its way into distinctly un-Thai dishes in our household – very good in a toasted cheese sandwich or as a glaze for roasted chicken. I made this version with fresh chillies although it is just as common to use dried chillies, toasting them to darken the skin before grinding them into the paste.

120 ml/½ cup vegetable oil

3 large shallots, chopped

3 garlic cloves, chopped

a pinch of sea salt

3 Thai chillies, deseeded and roughly chopped

½ teaspoon shrimp paste (gapi)

2 tablespoons ground dried shrimp

1½ tablespoons fish sauce, or to taste

2 teaspoons palm sugar, or to taste

1 teaspoon tamarind paste, or to taste

Heat a small wok over medium heat and add 2 tablespoons of the oil. Fry the shallots and garlic for 5 minutes, or until softened and translucent. Put them into a mortar and pound with a pestle into a smooth paste. Add the salt and chillies and repeat the process. Add the shrimp paste and dried shrimp. Continue pounding until you have a fine, uniform paste.

Put the remaining oil in the wok and heat over medium heat. Reduce the heat and add the paste. Fry gently to allow the ingredients to combine their flavours. Season with the fish sauce, palm sugar and tamarind paste to taste. Mix well and remove from the heat.

Store in an airtight sterilized container in the fridge.

I would use this: in stir-fries, as a dip for homemade pork crackling or in classic Thai Tom Yam Gung soup.

"Sour Orange" Curry Paste (opposite: right)

Unlike the sour orange pastes and marinades of Central America, this Thai curry paste is so called because of its colour, not because of the presence of sour oranges.

Thai pastes are generally pounded together in a mortar beginning with the ingredients that will take the most work to reduce to a pulp, then adding further ingredients in a logical sequence until everything is reduced to a smooth paste. They are simple to make, although often time consuming and a little tiring! However, the individual characteristics this method produces make up for the extra effort. You could, of course, decide to blitz everything together in a blender, and this would produce a very delicious and useable version of a Thai paste, but I would urge you to do it the hard way at least once. The difference can be astonishing. It is worth remembering two things: the larger and heavier the pestle and mortar you use the easier the process will be; and a good wrist technique will always produce better results more quickly than using brute force.

5–6 dried long red Cayenne-style chillies, deseeded and soaked in warm water or vinegar for 20 minutes

3 whole dried red Bird's Eye chillies, stalks removed

½ teaspoon sea salt

1 lemongrass stalk, tough outer leaves removed, finely chopped

2 Bird's Eye chillies, deseeded and chopped

1 large or 2 small red shallots, finely chopped

1 teaspoon shrimp paste

1 teaspoon tamarind paste

Remove the chillies from their soaking liquid and squeeze out the excess moisture, then chop finely. Heat a small frying pan over medium heat and briefly toast the whole dried Bird's Eye chillies until they just begin to colour.

Put the Cayenne chillies and dried Bird's Eye chillies into a mortar and add the salt. Using a pestle, pound the chillies until they have formed a smooth paste. Add the lemongrass and repeat the process. Do this with each ingredient in turn, making sure you have a smooth paste before adding the next ingredient.

The finished paste will be very hot, sour and vividly coloured.

I would use this: with coconut milk, fish sauce and palm sugar to make the perfect hot Thai curry sauce for white fish.

Nuoc Cham, Ho Chi Minh-style (below: left)

Vietnamese cuisine is perhaps the most exciting emerging cuisine at the moment, and it is often considered to be the healthiest of the South-East Asian diets. My original version of Nuoc Cham has evolved here to incorporate some other wonderful flavours, ending up as a distinctly southern Vietnamese version of Nuoc Cham. This version is particularly good with beef and noodle salads.

1 small lime

2 garlic cloves, crushed

2.5-cm/1-inch piece fresh ginger, peeled and very finely chopped

2 small hot green chillies, deseeded and finely chopped

50 ml/scant ¼ cup coconut water

2 teaspoons unrefined (golden caster) sugar

2 tablespoons Vietnamese-style fish sauce (or Thai fish sauce, to taste)

Squeeze the juice from the lime into a small bowl and set aside. Scrape the pulp from the lime into a mortar. Add the garlic, ginger and chillies and pound, using a pestle, to form a paste. If you find it difficult to pound this to a paste the ingredients could be briefly pulsed in a food processor to achieve the desired consistency.

Add the coconut water and sugar to the bowl of lime juice and stir to dissolve the sugar. Scrape the paste into the bowl with the lime juice mixture, add the fish sauce and mix well. (Vietnamese fish sauce is lighter in style than traditional nam pla – Thai fish sauce. If you are unable to source the Vietnamese sauce, Thai-style fish sauce works well, but you may wish to reduce the quantity slightly or add it gradually to taste.)

I would use this: to flavour noodles, grilled/broiled beef, rice and salads.

Tuong Goi Cuon (Vietnamese Peanut Sauce) (opposite: right)

Possibly, Tuong Goi Cuon is the perfect dipping sauce for serving with spring rolls. The recipe itself is incredibly simple, but it can be embellished in many ways to suit your personal taste. A truly authentic recipe in its simplest form uses water and vinegar with crushed peanuts added at the end; however, I think the finest version I have ever tasted uses pork stock instead of water, with tamarind as a souring agent instead of vinegar, and 1–2 tablespoons of peanut butter to every 4 tablespoons of hoisin! The point is, I am not convinced that these recipes should be set in stone. I think that making subtle changes and trying your own ideas reinvigorates recipes and can produce wonderful new tastes. It is good to start with an authentic recipe, but where you finally end up is part of the joy of cooking. This is the sauce I like!

180 ml/¾ cup warm pork stock, such as the cooking liquor from boiling a ham (or water)

4 tablespoons hoisin sauce

1–2 tablespoons peanut butter

2 tablespoons tamarind paste or vinegar, plus extra tamarind for seasoning, if needed

2 teaspoons soy sauce

½ teaspoon cornflour/ cornstarch

1 tablespoon vegetable oil

1 red shallot, finely chopped

4 garlic cloves, 3 finely chopped and 1 crushed

1 hot red chilli, such as Thai or Bird's Eye, deseeded and finely chopped

a pinch of palm sugar, if needed

Vietnamese fish sauce, if needed, or to taste (or Thai fish sauce, to taste)

a small handful of roasted unsalted peanuts

Pour the stock into a small bowl and add the hoisin sauce, peanut butter, tamarind, soy sauce and cornflour. Combine well using a fork or chopsticks.

Heat the oil in a small frying pan over high heat and quickly fry the shallot for 8 minutes, or until golden brown and crispy. (If you do not have a small frying pan you may need to use a little more oil to recreate the effect of deep-frying.) Remove the fried shallot and drain on kitchen paper/ paper towels.

Tip out most of the oil, leaving about 1 teaspoon in the pan, and put over medium heat. Add the 3 chopped garlic cloves and fry briefly until they just begin to colour, then stir in the chilli. While stirring the garlic mixture constantly, pour the contents of the small bowl into the pan, and continue stirring until the mixture comes to the boil. Remove from the heat and taste – the sauce should be slightly sweet, but sour and distinctly savoury too. Season with palm sugar to add sweetness, if needed, Vietnamese fish sauce, for saltiness (you will need less if using Thai fish sauce), and tamarind paste to increase the essential "sour" element. Crush the peanuts in a mortar using a pestle.

To serve, transfer the peanut sauce to a serving bowl and add the crushed garlic and peanuts. Stir well, then sprinkle with the fried shallots. Serve at room temperature.

I would use this: for dipping fresh spring rolls, or with simple fish and rice dishes.

Korean Chilli Marinade for Beef

In Korean restaurants, very thin strips of beef are marinated in this classic combination, then cooked on hot coals at the table and often served with a fermented soy bean, chilli and rice condiment – kochujang.

2 tablespoons sesame seeds

4 spring onions/scallions, sliced

2 green Finger chillies, thinly sliced diagonally

2 garlic cloves, very thinly sliced

5-cm/2-inch piece fresh ginger, peeled and finely chopped

4 tablespoons dark soy sauce

1 tablespoon nut oil

1 tablespoon rice wine vinegar

2 teaspoons palm sugar

Put the sesame seeds in a small saucepan over medium heat and toast until lightly golden, shaking the pan frequently. Tip into a serving bowl and add the remaining ingredients. Combine thoroughly.

I would use this: as a marinade for thin strips of beef. The beef will need at least 1 hour to marinate.

Kimchi (opposite)

For my 38th birthday I was taken out in Glasgow for a proper night out. We ended up eating in an extremely authentic Korean restaurant. I am ashamed to say that it was my first real experience of Korean food, and to this day I can't really recall most of the dishes we ate, but it did introduce me to the wonders of kimchi: a wonderfully spicy pickled cabbage that went well with everything. Making kimchi for the first time is a bit of a worry, as it goes against most of the fundamental things we are taught about preserving anything – rather like the Thai habit of boiling coconut milk until it separates, it is just not how you expect to do something. Take heart, though, because the end result is not only delicious but healthy too. Try it with any rice dishes.

4 tablespoons sea salt

500 g/1 lb. 2 oz. Chinese cabbage or pak choi, chopped into 2.5-cm/1-inch slices

100 g/3½ oz. shallots, roughly chopped

½ daikon radish or 4 large red radishes, quartered lengthways and cut into 1-cm/½-inch chunks

4 garlic cloves, crushed

5-cm/2-inch piece fresh ginger, peeled and grated

3 spring onions/scallions, very finely chopped

1 tablespoon dried chilli flakes

1 tablespoon dried Japanese kelp/seaweed (optional)

500-ml/2-cup kilner-style jar with non-reactive lid

Pour 1 litre/4 cups water into a bowl, add the salt and stir until the salt has dissolved. This is the brine.

Put the cabbage, shallots and radish in a large bowl and cover with the brine. Cover and leave overnight in the fridge.

The next day, put the garlic in a mortar with the ginger, spring onions/scallions and chilli flakes. Pound with a pestle to make a paste. Add the seaweed, if using. Drain the vegetables and return them to the large bowl. If the vegetables taste excessively salty, rinse them once with cold water and return them to the bowl. Add the garlic paste and mix thoroughly with the vegetables, ensuring that everything is coated.

Pack this mixture tightly into the kilner-style jar. Ideally, Kimchi ferments under pressure, so if you can find a suitable tea cup or bowl that can be put on top of the vegetable mixture to compress it when the lid is closed, this would be ideal. Place in a cool spot, but not the fridge, for 3–4 days. It is a good idea to open the jar daily and give the mixture a gentle stir before resealing. This avoids the build up of pressure in the sealed container as the vegetables ferment and ensures everything is well coated throughout the process.

The kimchi is ready when the mixture tastes a little sour and the cabbage has begun to soften and look translucent. At this point remove the cup, seal the jar and transfer to the fridge. This will halt the fermentation process. Serve by draining the water and bringing the kimchi to room temperature.

I would use this: as a fantastic addition to any rice dish. It can be drizzled with a little sesame oil to serve. It will keep well in the fridge and is past its best when it begins to smell sweet or vaguely alcoholic.

Sambals are very satisfying to make and provide a great flavour resource for impromptu dishes when you just don't know what you want to make! There are well over 300 different sambal recipes, just from Indonesia, so if you enjoy the process, there are many to experiment with — some cooked and some raw. These recipes are some of my favourites and suitably HOT!

Sambal Balado (opposite: left)

10 hot green chillies, thinly sliced
½ teaspoon sea salt
3 garlic cloves, finely chopped
2 shallots, finely chopped
1 red (or green) tomato, deseeded
juice of 1 lemon
1 tablespoon vegetable oil

Put the chillies and salt in a mortar and grind using a pestle. Add each remaining ingredient individually (except the oil) and pound between additions to make a uniform and slightly chunky paste.

Heat the oil in a wok and gently fry the paste until the ingredients are cooked through. They will lose their sharp, raw taste and the paste will become a little sweeter. Pour into a small bowl and allow to cool.

Sambal Oelek (opposite: right)

10 hot red chillies, such as Bird's Eye, stalks removed
½ teaspoon sea salt
½ teaspoon blachan shrimp paste
1 tablespoon usweetened tamarind paste or lime juice

Put the chillies and salt in a large mortar and pound into a smooth purée with a pestle. Add the shrimp paste and continue to grind together until completely mixed. Add the tamarind and grind until you have a smooth red paste.

Sambal Kacang (above: bottom)

150 g/1¼ cups deep-fried
   peanuts (or roasted salted
   peanuts)

1 small shallot, finely chopped

2 garlic cloves, chopped

4 Bird's Eye chillies, deseeded
   and chopped

1 kaffir lime leaf, finely
   chopped

2½ tablespoons ketjap manis
   – sweet dark soy (or
   2 tablespoons dark soy
   sauce plus 1 teaspoon sugar)

½ teaspoon sea salt

500 ml/2 cups water

2 teaspoons lime juice

Put the peanuts in a mortar and grind using a pestle. Add the shallot and pound into a paste. Repeat with the garlic and chillies, making sure each forms a thick paste before adding the next.

Tip the paste into a saucepan and add the lime leaf, ketjap manis, salt and water. Bring to a gentle simmer and cook for 1 hour, stirring occasionally, or until most of the water has evaporated. Stir in the lime juice, then allow to cool and serve.

Nasi Goreng Spice Paste and Blachan

Literally, Nasi Goreng means "fried rice", and the dish is unofficially the national dish of Indonesia. Originally, it was a way of using up leftover rice and meat or fish, but it is now often used to describe even the most complex fried-rice dish. This paste provides the spicy flavouring that is the heart of any good nasi goreng dish. Blachan is a dark shrimp paste that is surprisingly easy to make. Below is a simple recipe if you want to try making your own.

25 g/¼ cup roasted salted peanuts

2 tablespoons vegetable oil

4 large garlic cloves, roughly chopped

2 shallots, chopped

6 red chillies, roughly chopped

1 teaspoon blachan (dark shrimp paste)

1 teaspoon salt

Put the peanuts in a food processor and briefly blitz them. Add the remaining ingredients and process until you have thick paste – be sure to scrape down the sides of the bowl to ensure everything is evenly mixed.

You can store this paste in an airtight container in the fridge, but it is better to make it fresh as required.

I would use this: with any fried rice dish, or to coat chicken before cooking. See also page 136.

To make blachan (if you fancy it!)

100 g/3½ oz. dried shrimp powder

40 g/scant ½ cup desiccated coconut

2 small onions, chopped

5 garlic cloves, chopped

2.5-cm/1-inch piece fresh ginger, peeled and chopped

150 ml/scant ⅔ cup lemon juice

3 teaspoons chilli powder

sea salt

Toast the shrimp powder in a frying pan over low heat for 1–2 minutes, stirring constantly – be careful not to allow the powder to burn. Pour into a bowl and allow to cool.

Briefly toast the desiccated coconut in the frying pan, stirring constantly, until it has turned a rich golden colour, being careful not to allow it to burn. Pour into a separate bowl to cool.

Put the remaining ingredients into a food processor or blender and blend to a thick, smooth paste. Add the shrimp paste and coconut, and continue to blend, adding a little water as required to make a thick paste. Season with salt to taste. Pack into an airtight container and store in the fridge.

Malay Curry Powder

I must admit that I encountered this curry powder not in Malaysia but in Cape Town, South Africa. It was used as a dry rub for meat before being placed on the ubiquitous Braai. It is exceptionally good with fish and chicken, although it is also great as the base powder for my favourite pheasant and prune curry. I used this curry powder to make the sauce for Pinang Kerrie Sauce (page 45).

3 dried red Bird's Eye chillies, deseeded

5-cm/2-inch piece cinnamon stick, roughly broken up

2 teaspoons Szechuan peppercorns

½ piece star anise

1 teaspoon coriander seeds

1 teaspoon fennel seeds

5 cloves

seeds from 1 green cardamom pod

2–3 dried kaffir lime leaves, roughly broken up

a good grating of fresh nutmeg

2 teaspoons ground turmeric

Put the chillies in a heavy-based saucepan over medium heat and add the cinnamon, peppercorns, star anise, coriander seeds, fennel seeds and cloves. Toast until they begin to release their aroma. Add the cardamom seeds and toast for another 30 seconds.

Tip the toasted spices into a mortar or spice grinder. Add the lime leaves and grind to a fine powder. Tip into a bowl and add the nutmeg and turmeric, then mix together thoroughly. Transfer to a sealable container until you are ready to use it.

I would use this: to cook with fish or pheasant. See also pages 45 and 147.

Nasi Goreng (The Perfect Cooked Breakfast)

I really love breakfast, but the reality is that if offered a bowl of cereal or a dry slice of toast, I would genuinely rather not bother. I think this is because it is so half-hearted. Like any other meal, if you are going to have breakfast, why not do it properly? With this aim in mind, the idea of a cooked breakfast is one to be celebrated — especially one that has a little hint of chilli. Chilli gives the body a wonderful wake-up call in the morning — just ask Jamie Oliver, who regularly nibbles a fresh chilli first thing in the morning. Here I celebrate what is practically the national dish in Indonesia: nasi goreng. it makes a fantastic breakfast, and if you want a little more heat, just add a couple of finely sliced chillies into the wok when you're cooking the garlic.

1½ tablespoons Nasi Goreng Spice Paste (page 134)

a handful of raw tiger prawns/shrimp

2 tablespoons vegetable oil

1 shallot, finely sliced

1 garlic clove, finely chopped

225 g/1½ cups cooked rice

2 teaspoons ketjap manis – sweet dark soy, plus extra to serve (optional)

1 teaspoon tomato purée/paste

a good pinch of palm sugar

2 small spring onions/scallions, finely chopped

1 egg

cucumber and tomatoes, to serve, plus sliced chillies (optional)

Serves 1

Put ½ tablespoon of the Nasi Goreng Spice Paste in a bowl. Add the prawns/shrimp and mix together to coat them — add a little oil if required to do this. Set aside for 20 minutes in the fridge.

Heat the oil in a wok or frying pan over medium heat. Add the shallot and garlic and fry for 1 minute. Add the remaining Nasi Goreng Spice Paste and fry for a few minutes until the paste cooks and becomes aromatic. Tip in the rice and stir well to ensure it is evenly covered in the spicy paste. Add the ketjap manis, tomato purée/paste and palm sugar and continue to fry, stirring constantly. Add the onions and prawns/shrimp and cook until the prawns/shrimp turn pink and are cooked through. Transfer to a serving plate. Keep warm.

Add a little more oil to the wok and heat over medium heat. Break the egg into the oil and fry until the edges begin to brown. Either spoon some of the oil over the egg to ensure even cooking, or flip the egg if you prefer.

To serve, place the egg on top of the nasi goreng and dress the plate with the slices of cucumber and tomato. Extra ketjap manis or fresh sliced chillies can be used a condiments.

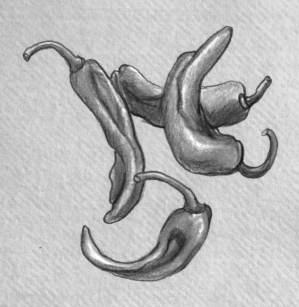

Noted Chillies: Shishito (pictured here), Takanotsume, Japone, Chi-Chen, Hainan Yellow Lantern and Facing Heaven (still commercially grown in China!).

Chilli Facts and Fiction: Not surprisingly, chillies are regularly used in traditional medicine in China. Research there has shown success in treating conditions such as angina and high blood pressure.

Chapter Eight

China & Japan

When it comes to production of fresh chilli nowhere even comes close to China, which regularly produces more the 12,000,000 tonnes of fresh chillies per annum, and this figure has been growing at an average of 9.7% since the mid-nineties. Interestingly, if India, which is comfortably the largest producer of dried chillies, decided to sell these as fresh, by weight, it would produce in excess of 40,000,000 tonnes per annum!

- Despite being considerably smaller than China, Japan is still a major producer of fresh chillies and is incredibly efficient with a yield per acre of more than double that of China and 4 times that of India.

- Commercially grown chillies in China are not given names but are nearly all specifically bred hybrids. The most common is Xiangyan 19 although Xiangyan 1 through to 21 are also grown. This is something that causes keen growers of slightly odder varieties of chilli a great deal of anxiety; if these hybrids are ideally suited to their growing conditions they will soon displace some of the varieties we consider to be indigenous to China and if they are bred to suit chilli growing conditions how will we stop them spreading into other contiguous areas such as India? Perhaps the most astonishing thing is that all this is just being done to feed the ever-growing demand for chillies – plants that 500 years ago only existed in a relatively confined area of Central and South America.

- Japan still commercially grows a number of "native" varieties, most of which are extremely rare outside its borders.

Red Chilli Oil (opposite: right)

This is a classic Chinese ingredient, an integral part of Szechuan cooking and the perfect accompaniment to pork wontons! It is hot, and it gets hotter the longer it is stored. Great modifications include reducing the chilli and adding a few bruised garlic cloves. This is a fragrant oil for use in cooking and dressings.

500 ml/2 cups vegetable oil or groundnut oil (avoid olive oil or strongly flavoured oils)

2 spring onions/scallions, bruised with the back of a knife

a thumb-sized piece fresh ginger, bruised with the back of a heavy knife or rolling pin

100 g/3½ oz. dried chilli flakes

2 teaspoons Szechuan peppercorns

2 star anise

Heat the oil, onions and ginger in a medium saucepan over medium-high heat until the oil just begins to smoke. Remove from the heat and remove the onions from the oil. Set aside to cool a little.

Put the chilli flakes, peppercorns and star anise in medium ceramic bowl. Remove the ginger from the oil and pour the still-hot oil into the bowl. With a metal/ceramic spoon, give everything a good mix. Leave overnight for the flavours to infuse. The chilli, star anise and peppercorns should settle to the bottom of the bowl. Carefully pour the oil into a sterilized bottle, being careful not to disturb the sediment in the bottom of the bowl. I often strain the oil through a funnel lined with coffee filter paper to be sure to get all the oil and none of the flavouring ingredients. Seal tightly and store in a cool dark place for several months.

I would use this: to make Szechuan dipping sauce or to spice up noodles.

Szechuan Red and Black Dipping Sauce (opposite: left)

This is a lovely way to use your homemade Red Chilli Oil. It is worth trying to find black vinegar for this recipe; it is a fragrant, slightly alcoholic rice vinegar that adds an indefinable oriental quality to dishes.

2 tablespoons Red Chilli Oil (see above)

1 tablespoon Chinese black vinegar (Chinkiang vinegar) or balsamic vinegar

3 tablespoons soy sauce

½ tablespoon sesame oil

½ teaspoon ground Szechuan pepper

½ teaspoon sugar

1 garlic clove, crushed

1 tablespoon finely grated or shredded fresh ginger

1 spring onion/scallion, finely chopped

In a small bowl, mix the Red Chilli Oil, vinegar, soy sauce and sesame oil. Add the pepper and sugar and mix to dissolve the sugar. Add the remaining ingredients and stir through until everything is mixed evenly together. Set aside for an hour to allow the flavours to infuse.

I would use this: with prawn/shrimp dumplings, beef or chicken gyoza, or Szechuan wontons.

Chinese Pickled Green Chillies

This is another must-have kitchen staple. I would definitely encourage you to make your own pickled chillies, as they are so much nicer than storebought ones.

120 g/4 oz. bullet-style hot green chillies or Jalapeños, sliced

100 ml/scant ½ cup boiling water

250 ml/1 cup Shaoxing rice wine

1 tablespoon sugar

1 teaspoon sea salt

4 Szechuan peppercorns

½ star anise

Put the chillies in a bowl and pour the boiling water over them. After about 30 seconds, drain the chillies. Lay them on some kitchen paper/paper towels and pat them dry.

Heat the vinegar in a small saucepan, add the sugar and salt and stir until dissolved. Heat until it just comes to the boil.

Put the chillies in a sterilized container with a tightly fitting lid along with the peppercorns and the star anise. Pour the hot vinegar solution into the jar, ensuring that the chillies are covered. Seal the jar and give a quick shake. Allow to cool. Leave for at least 1 week: the longer the better!

I would use this: as a perfect side dish for stir fries or noodle dishes.

Hunan Chilli Sauce

The Hunan region of China is known for its intensely spicy cuisine. It is also a hugely important region in the production of chillies themselves. It has even lent its name to the unbearable burning sensation you get from handling too many chillies without protection: "Hunan Hand". In fact, in Hunan the most common symptoms presented by patients at medical centres are all related to over-exposure to capsaicin, the odourless, tasteless compound that gives chillies their heat.

This sauce is extremely hot and is in fact as much a pickle as a sauce. It is used in numerous recipes from Hunan including the infamous fish head soup!

100 g/3½ oz. fresh hot red chillies, deseeded and chopped

1 small ripe pear, peeled, cored and roughly chopped

4 garlic cloves, crushed

5-cm/2-inch piece fresh ginger, peeled and very finely chopped

1–2 teaspoons sea salt

2 tablespoons Shaoxing rice wine

Put all the ingredients in a blender or food processor and pulse until smooth but thick. Transfer to a bowl and leave for 10–15 minutes.

Check the seasoning (it will be very spicy!) and add more salt or vinegar as required. Spoon the mixture into a sterilized glass jar, pressing it down to pack it into the jar. Leave a space of about 3 cm/1¼ inches at the top of the jar. Top up the jar with a little more rice wine vinegar to ensure that the paste is entirely covered. Seal the jar and store somewhere moderately cool and dark for a minimum of 20 days after which the sauce will be ready to use – with great care!

I would use this: in any classic hot and sour Hunan dish to provide the "hot"! See also page 148.

Szechuan Chilli Paste

What do you get if you put 3 cooks in a room and give them a recipe for something they have never made before? The answer is normally 3 totally unrelated dishes! However if you don't give them a recipe, just ingredients, and you get 3 dishes that taste the same, something at least is right – and this is what we got here. We wanted to try to represent the flavours of the region using the simplest selection of ingredients we could find; as a result we didn't even ferment broad/fava beans, much to my disappointment. Facing Heaven chillies are readily available from Chinese supermarkets and add a distinct quality to this paste that is worth the extra effort involved in finding them.

1 tablespoon vegetable oil

1 teaspoon toasted sesame oil

5 garlic cloves, finely chopped

3-cm/1¼-inch piece fresh ginger, peeled and finely chopped

1 onion, finely chopped

3 hot red chillies, deseeded and finely sliced

3 Facing Heaven chillies, deseeded

2 vine-ripened tomatoes, finely chopped

3 tablespoons Shaoxing rice wine

½ teaspoon Szechuan pepper, freshly ground

1 teaspoon sea salt

1 tablespoon sugar

2 tablespoons Shaoxing rice wine

Heat both varieties of oil in a wok over high heat and fry the garlic and ginger for a few moments, stirring continuously. Add the onion and fry for a further 1 minute. Add the chillies and tomatoes and cook for a further 1 minute, then add the vinegar. Reduce the heat and simmer for 5 minutes.

Add the pepper, salt, sugar and rice wine and simmer until the ingredients are all cooked. Blitz to a smooth purée with a blender, food processor or stick blender. Transfer the paste to an airtight container and allow to cool. Allow the flavours to mingle for about 48 hours before using.

I would use this: to add a little kick to any Chinese meal or to flavour simple rice and noodle dishes.

Hunan-style Chilli and Black Bean Sauce

Again this recipe pays tribute to the Hunan love of HEAT. Traditionally it is always cooked by steaming; completely sealing the bowl using clingfilm/plastic wrap before foil is a great way of ensuring that none of the flavour escapes in the cooking process!

3 tablespoons sunflower oil

4 garlic cloves, crushed

2 tablespoons dried chilli flakes (or more if you like things hotter!)

2 teaspoons Shaoxing rice wine

1 teaspoon toasted sesame oil

1 tablespoon fermented black beans, rinsed

a large pinch of sea salt

Put all the ingredients in a heatproof glass or ceramic bowl. Mix together thoroughly. Cover with a sheet of clingfilm/plastic wrap and then tightly with a sheet of foil.

Place a steamer over a pan of boiling water and set the sealed bowl in the steamer. Place the lid on the steamer – or if the bowl is too big, cover it with a couple of layers of foil. Allow to steam for about 45 minutes, regularly checking the water level and topping it up with boiling water if required. Remove from the heat and allow to cool.

Serve immediately or refrigerate until needed, then allow to come to room temperature before serving.

I would use this: in spicy prawn/shrimp or chicken dishes.

Szechuan Chicken Marinade

Szechuan pepper is extremely interesting; although not hot, it has a distinct lemon aroma and can produce a somewhat strange tingly (sometimes numbing) sensation in the mouth. This makes it the perfect partner to hot spices in a marinade or sauce; in many respects it has the perfect home in Szechuan cuisine.

1 tablespoon vegetable oil

1 large onion, chopped

2 garlic cloves, chopped

3-cm/1¼-inch piece fresh ginger, peeled and chopped

½–1 Habanero chilli, deseeded and finely chopped

2 tablespoons sugar

2 tablespoons dark soy sauce

2 tablespoons Shaoxing rice wine

2 tablespoons rice vinegar or white wine vinegar

½ teaspoon black peppercorns, 1 teaspoon Szechuan pepper and ½ teaspoon sea salt, ground together with a mortar and pestle

water, as required

Heat the oil in a wok and fry the onion, garlic and ginger until softened. Transfer to a food processor with the chilli, sugar, soy sauce, rice wine and rice vinegar. Blend to a smooth paste, adding a little water if required.

Return the paste to the wok with the ground pepper mixture and gently heat. Stir and cook until it comes to the boil, then reduce the heat and gently simmer for about 5 minutes, adding water if the paste becomes too thick. It should have the consistency of a thin purée. Taste and season further if required.

Remove from the heat and allow to cool to room temperature. Allow your chosen meat to marinate in this for a minimum of 2 hours.

I would use this: with chicken or maybe even pheasant.

Chinese Curry Sauce (An English Takeout Treatment!)

This is a recipe that you will either see as a travesty or a triumph. Either way, it is full of classic ingredients and makes a fantastic base for chicken curry. It shows its real versatility when allowed to thicken a little and used as a dip for proper British chip-shop chips! Having grown up in London and the southwest England, the idea of curry sauce or any sauce with chips was frankly disturbing. But it has its place, and when you find that place the pleasure to be derived is enormous! I also like mushy peas before you ask...

2 tablespoons vegetable oil

1 onion, finely chopped

3–4 garlic cloves, crushed

5-cm/2-inch piece fresh ginger, peeled and finely chopped (or ideally microplaned)

1 tablespoon Malay Curry Powder (page 135)

2 tablespoons plain/all-purpose flour

½ teaspoon black peppercorns, finely ground

½ teaspoon paprika

½ teaspoon Chinese five-spice

1 tablespoon oyster sauce

1 teaspoon light soy sauce

warm water, as required

a large pinch of sugar

sea salt, to taste

Heat the oil in a saucepan over medium heat. Gently fry the onion, stirring regularly, until it begins to soften. Add the garlic and ginger and fry for another couple of minutes.

Stir in the Malay Curry Powder and flour and fry for 2–3 minutes, stirring to stop the ingredients sticking to the pan. Now add the pepper, paprika, five-spice, oyster sauce and soy sauce. Continue cooking and mixing to make a thick paste. Gradually add warm water, stirring continuously to blend the water with the paste until you have a reached a consistency similar to thick gravy.

Add the sugar and bring to the boil. Reduce the heat and simmer for 3–5 minutes, allowing the sauce to thicken just a little. Season to taste with salt.

I would use this: as a base for a Chinese chicken curry. Or let it thicken a little more when cooking and it is the perfect curry sauce for dipping fries into!

Hunan Chilli Marinated Fish

If I think of something really spicy, packed with chilli-heat and flavours, it is always a fish dish. It is often thought that fish is too delicate for big, robust flavours but if you look at classic bold dishes like bouillabaisse, teriyaki, Caribbean fish stew, Creole jambalaya and so on, they more often than not use fish, shellfish and seafood as their main protein. As we have already discovered, Hunan is the chilli capital of China. Its sub-tropical climate with hot, humid summers makes it ideal for growing chillies as well as most other fruit and vegetables. The real secret to the cuisine of this region though is Lake Dongting. Situated in the centre of Hunan it is the second largest lake in China and provides much of the fish used in the varied cuisine of this landlocked province. The recipe below calls for firm white fish, which to be truly authentic would undoubtedly be freshwater fish. If this is hard to come by, a good fishmonger should be able to sell you some zander (or pike or perch), which would be ideal.

1 tablespoon Hunan Chilli Sauce (page 143), plus extra to serve (optional)

3 tablespoons soy sauce

1 tablespoon Shaoxing rice wine

2-cm/1-inch piece fresh ginger, peeled and finely chopped

2 garlic cloves, crushed

1 shallot, very finely chopped

700 g/1½ lbs. fresh firm white fish, cut into 5-cm/2-inch cubes

nut oil, for deep-frying

2 eggs, lightly beaten

100–125 g/2 cups fine, fresh breadcrumbs

250 ml/1 cup chicken stock

3 tablespoons sugar

1 small Romano-style red sweet/bell pepper, deseeded and very finely chopped

cooked rice or noodles, to serve

Chinese Pickled Green Chillies (page 142), to serve (optional)

Serves 4 as a light main/entrée

Mix together the Hunan Chilli Sauce, soy sauce, rice wine, ginger, garlic and shallot. Place the fish cubes in a dish and pour the marinade over them, turning them to ensure they are evenly coated. Cover and marinate in the fridge for 30 minutes. Remove the fish from the bowl and reserve the marinade.

In a deep frying pan, pour in enough oil for deep-frying to reach a depth of about 2 cm/¾ inch. Heat over medium heat until the oil reaches about 180°C (350°F) – test by frying a small cube of bread; it should brown in 40 seconds.

Dip the fish into the beaten eggs, then coat evenly with breadcrumbs. Deep-fry in the hot oil in batches, turning the pieces regularly with tongs until evenly cooked and a rich golden colour. Remove from the pan, drain on kitchen paper/paper towels and keep warm.

Put the reserved marinade in a small saucepan with the chicken stock and sugar. Mix well and bring to the boil, stirring to dissolve the sugar. Turn down the heat and allow the sauce to reduce for about 10 minutes. (If you want to thicken the sauce, blend 1 tablespoon of cornflour/cornstarch with 1 tablespoon of water, briskly stir this into the pan and continue to cook.) A few minutes before the end of cooking, add the sweet/bell pepper.

Place the fish on a bed of cooked rice or noodles and pour the sauce over the top. Accompany with a little more Hunan Chilli Sauce, if you dare, or with some Chinese Pickled Green Chillies and soy sauce and a small glass of rice wine.

Japanese Curry Powder

Since the days of the Raj, the British have taken it upon themselves to spread curry around the world with evangelical zeal and so it is only moderately surprising to learn that curry was first introduced to Japan in the late 19th century by the British. Even the Imperial Japanese Navy adopted curry as its favourite dish from the British Navy. Curry rice is now ubiquitous throughout Japan and is generally made using an instant curry roux. This spice recipe just needs to be fried with oil and flour to make just such a roux. Loosen with water and served over plain steamed rice for an unexpected taste of modern Japan.

3 tablespoons ground turmeric

2 tablespoons ground coriander

1 tablespoon ground cumin

1 teaspoon ground cardamom

1 teaspoon freshly ground black pepper

½ teaspoon cayenne pepper

½ teaspoon ground fennel seeds

¼ teaspoon ground cloves

¼ teaspoon ground bay

a large pinch of grated nutmeg

a large pinch of ground cinnamon

2 dried sage leaves, rubbed to a powder

Put all the ingredients in a jar, shake to mix, then seal tightly. Store in a cool, dark place until required.

I would use this: mixed with oil and flour in a hot saucepan to make a classic Japanese curry sauce.

Chilli Pickled Ginger

Pickled ginger (and pickled garlic for that matter) are delights that you can only enjoy when you reach a certain age. I have tried so many times to secrete these in otherwise entirely acceptable kids' sandwich combinations only to find them picked out and discarded later. I am sure I would have been the same at that age had these delights been available then. However, once you embrace pickles there is no going back... that reminds me – pickled eggs!

250 g/9 oz. fresh ginger, avoiding any tough or dry, fibrous roots as much as possible

a kettle of boiling water

250 ml/1 cup Japanese rice vinegar

6 tablespoons sugar

½ tablespoon salt

5 medium-heat red bullet-style chillies, halved lengthways and deseeded

500-ml/2-cup kilner-style jar with non-reactive lid

Peel the ginger. Using a sharp knife (or mandoline if you have one), slice the ginger as thinly as you can. Put the sliced ginger in a large bowl and pour the boiling water over it. Give it a little stir. After about 30 seconds, drain it and lay the ginger slices on kitchen paper/paper towels. Pat dry with more kitchen paper/paper towels.

Pour the vinegar and sugar into a saucepan and bring to the boil over medium heat, stirring to dissolve the sugar. Add the salt and stir to dissolve. Now boil for about 30 seconds, then remove from the heat.

Put the ginger and chilli halves in the kilner-style jar. Pour over the vinegar solution, ensuring that the ginger and chillies are submerged. Seal the lid and allow to cool naturally. Store in a cool, dark place.

The ginger will be ready to eat in about 1 week but will keep quite happily in the fridge, even after opening, for 4–6 months.

I would use this: in salads and sandwiches, or on the side of any spicy dish. See also page 153.

Teriyaki Marinade (opposite)

Teriyaki is in fact more of a way of cooking than a recipe; in that sense it's a bit like Indian tandoori. In Japanese "yaki" means "to grill/broil" (or sometimes "roast") and "teri" means "sheen" or "lustre". So to cook something "teriyaki" means to grill/broil it with a lustrous or glazed surface. The key ingredient in achieving this sheen is mirin. Mirin is a kind of low-alcohol "sake". The most authentic sort of mirin is "hon" mirin; this literally translates as "true" mirin and has an alcohol content of 14%. "Shio" mirin is the other acceptable rice wine to use in teriyaki; it too contains alcohol but has salt added. This makes it undrinkable as wine and thus avoids the duty levied on alcohol!

1.5-cm/½-inch piece fresh ginger, peeled and finely grated, preferably microplaned

1 Shishito chilli, deseeded and very finely chopped

1 small garlic clove, crushed

3 tablespoons Tamari soy sauce

2 tablespoons "hon" mirin

1 tablespoon rice vinegar

2 teaspoons honey or brown sugar

Put the ginger, chilli and garlic into a mortar and pound with a pestle to a smooth paste. Add the liquid ingredients and blend together until everything is evenly mixed.

I would use this: with chicken or salmon. See also page 154.

Japanese Pickled Ginger Salad Dressing

You get a lovely hint of warmth from the homemade Chilli Pickled Ginger in this recipe. Do not limit this salad dressing to just Asian dishes – it is lovely over chicken salad and almost perfect with a finely chopped Russian salad of tuna, carrots, peas, potato, parsley and capers.

1 small onion, finely chopped

1 carrot, finely chopped

3 tablespoons soy sauce

2 tablespoons Japanese rice vinegar

1 tablespoon finely chopped Chilli Pickled Ginger (page 151)

2 teaspoons sugar

½ teaspoon freshly ground black pepper

2 teaspoon toasted sesame seeds

3 tablespoons groundnut oil

Put the onion, carrot, soy sauce, vinegar, Chilli Pickled Ginger, sugar, pepper and sesame seeds in a food processor or blender and blend to a smooth paste. Continue to blend while gradually adding the oil so that the mixture emulsifies. Serve immediately.

I would use this: as a dressing for a simple salad of gem lettuce, hard-boiled eggs and grated carrot.

Teriyaki Salmon with Soba Noodles and Crunchy Salad

This is a no-nonsense, simple Asian supper. The salmon should be moist, richly coloured and strongly flavoured, the salad crunchy and fresh, the dressing salty, sweet and sour and the noodles should provide the perfect backdrop, soaking up any escapee flavours! This teriyaki marinade will also work wonderfully well with chicken. Allow the meat to marinate for a minimum of 2 hours and alter the cooking time to ensure the chicken is cooked through. I would thickly slice the chicken diagonally and serve on the noodles with a generous dressing of more of the teriyaki sauce.

2 meaty salmon fillets, skin on

Teriyaki Marinade (page 153)

1 tablespoon soy sauce

1½ tablespoons fine palm sugar

1 teaspoon fish sauce

juice of 2 limes

2-cm/¾-inch piece fresh ginger, peeled and very finely julienned

1 red sweet/bell pepper, deseeded and finely julienned

a handful of Chinese cabbage, finely shredded

1 "supermarket" red chilli, deseeded and finely julienned

a small handful of coriander/cilantro, finely chopped

a small handful of beansprouts

125 g/4½ oz. soba noodles

2 spring onions/scallions, finely chopped

1 small medium-heat red chilli, deseeded and finely chopped

1 small carrot, grated

a drizzle of sesame oil

1 teaspoon toasted sesame seeds

Serves 2

Put the salmon fillets in a shallow dish and pour over the Teriyaki Marinade. Ensure all of the fish is well coated. Cover with clingfilm/plastic wrap and marinate in the fridge for about 30–45 minutes.

Make a salad dressing by mixing together the soy sauce, palm sugar, fish sauce and the juice of 1 lime.

In a large bowl, combine the ginger, sweet/bell pepper, cabbage, julienned chilli, coriander/cilantro and beansprouts. Toss with the salad dressing and set aside.

Cook the soba noodles according to the pack instructions and drain into a large bowl.

Preheat the grill/broiler to high. Cover a grill/broiler rack with foil and place the salmon, skin-side up, on the foil. Reserve the marinade. Grill/broil for 4–5 minutes, then turn the salmon over and spoon a generous quantity of the reserved marinade over the flesh side of the fish. Grill/broil for a further 4–5 minutes until the salmon if perfectly cooked. Turn the grill/broiler off and using the latent heat keep the salmon warm.

Add the onions, chopped chilli and carrot to the noodles. Squeeze over the juice of the remaining lime and drizzle with sesame oil. Toss together.

To serve, place a portion of noodles on the plate alongside a lustrous salmon fillet. Dress with a little more lime juice and scatter the sesame seeds over the top. Serve the salad alongside in a small side bowl.

Suppliers & Stockists

UK

This is a small representation of the wealth of chilli outlets and farms now doing business in the UK. For more information on the full range of UK suppliers why not visit www.chilefoundry.co.uk

Chillipepperpete

Chilli Pepper Pete and Fiery Foods UK offer an astonishingly broad range of chilli products from seeds and dried chillies (a really extensive range) through hot sauces and curry sauces to chilli gifts and treats. They also host the Fiery Foods chilli festivals in the UK and organize the UK National Chilli Awards!
www.chillipepperpete.com

Edible Ornamentals

Edible Ornamentals based in Bedfordshire operate the UK's first "Pick your own" chilli. In season over 40 varieties of chilli are available to pick fresh. Both fresh chillies and plants and an exciting range of their own products are also available from their online shop.
www.edibleornamentals.co.uk

Hot Headz

Run by Stuart McAllister, Hot Headz were the first specialist chilli retailer in the UK. They operate an excellent website selling not only their own products but a great range of sauces, salsas and chilli products from all over the world. Their smoked chilli and garlic hot sauce is one of my favourite chilli products ever!
www.hot-headz.com

Mr Vikki's

Check out Adam's chutneys, pickles, nuts and sauces, to name but a few lines. Based on the edge of the Lake District and hand-made, tasted, packed and shipped by the man himself. If you are in the Lake District be sure to visit them at Keswick Market.
www.mrvikkis.co.uk

Nicky's Nursery

Suppliers of an excellent and broad range of chilli seeds. They sell in excess of 200 varieties of chilli seeds via their website and I have found them to provide some of the most reliable seeds I have ever bought. In 2008 and 2009 "Which" awarded them a "Which Best Buy", further enhancing their reputation for quality.
www.nickys-nursery.co.uk

Scorchio

Now the UK's leading online chilli deli with a monstrous range of products from the UK and around the world. Loads to choose from and great service!
www.scorchio.co.uk

Sea Spring Seeds

Run by Joy and Michael Michaud Sea Spring Seeds sell an extremely well trialled and selective range of chilli seeds. They also operate Sea Spring Plants and Peppers by Post selling chilli plug plants and fresh chillies respectively. Sea Spring is the home to the now legendary Dorset Naga.
www.seaspringseeds.co.uk

Seasoned Pioneers

Endorsed by leading food writers and offering without doubt the most comprehensive range of specialist spice blends and seasonings available in the UK, Seasoned Pioneers are true to their word and represent every major worldwide cuisine and an awful lot that are not so major! If any spice, herb or blend is proving particularly elusive this is always my first port of call.
www.seasonedpioneers.co.uk

Simpsons Seeds

Located on the Longleat Estate in Wiltshire Simpson's Seeds provide a great range of chilli seeds from their own nursery. Matt Simpson has also written an excellent book on growing chillies: "Chilli, Chili, Chile: Peppers Sweet and Hot". The nursery in open from April each year but their seed shop is open all year round. Seeds can also be purchased from their website.
www.simpsonsseeds.co.uk

South Devon Chilli Farm

Opened in 2003 South Devon Chilli Farm is run by Jason Nickels and Steve Waters. Over 2 sites they grow in excess of 10,000 chilli plants per year. Their Loddiswell site has a small shop open 7 days a week. They also have an excellent online shop which sells a broad range of their products including fresh chillies from July to November.
www.southdevonchillifarm.co.uk

Spicy Monkey

Handmade curry pastes, spice mixes and marinades from the northeast of England – the spiritual home of chilli!
www.spicymonkey.co.uk

The Chile Seed Company
Founded and run by Gerald Fowler, this Cumbrian-based business sells an extraordinary array of chilli seeds as well as a good range of their own products. They can also be found at nearly any UK event with chilli in the title!
www.chileseeds.co.uk

The Chilli Jam Man
Simon makes a wonderful range of chilli jams. Made with great passion and enthusiasm they are some of the best British chilli products out there.
www.thechillijamman.com

Upton Cheyney Chilli Company
One of my favourite new chilli companies and located between Bath and Bristol, their growing and manufacture really embrace the field to fork ethos! They even hold their own chilli festival on the farm at the beginning of September.
www.uptonchilli.co.uk

Wiltshire Chilli Farm
As with most great ideas Wiltshire Chilli Farm was dreamt up in the pub. A relative newcomer in the UK, having started growing in February 2010. They have grown quickly and now operate from 4200 sq. ft. of growing space.
www.justchillies.co.uk/wiltshire chillies/

US

Kalustyan's
Online groceries, including a huge range of dried chillies, spices, ground peppers and more. Eg sweet smoked paprika (pimentón dulce) and Piquillo peppers.
www.kalustyans.com

La Tienda
Stockists of the best Spanish produce including fresh Padron peppers, roasted Piquillo peppers and sweet smoked paprika (pimentón dulce).
www.tienda.com

Marx Foods
Mostly commercial supplier, but they have a good stock of fresh, dried and ground/crushed chillies.
www.marxfoods.com

Melissa's
Great source for hard-to-find fresh produce including dozens of different chillies.
www.melissas.com

New Mexican Connection
For all fresh and dried New Mexican favourites.
www.newmexicanconnection.com

Penzeys Spices
Ground Ancho, smoked Chipotles, Piquin, galangal, and all manner of spices, herbs and seasonings.
www.penzeys.com

Tierra Vegetables
Brother and sister Wayne and Lee James have been farming 20 acres in the heart of the Sonoma Country Wine Country, 70 miles north of San Francisco, since 1979. In addition to growing a market garden, they also grow more than 20 varieties of chillies and sweet peppers. They also sell dried chillies.
www.tierravegetables.com

World Spice
Seattle's premier spice, herb and tea shop with a great online collection of whole or ground dried spices, including Piment d'Espelette. They also stock dried Mexican oregano, Baharat spice blend and Ras el Hanout.
www.worldspice.com

Index

achiote paste, Yucatecan 19
adobo mojado 64
ají amarillo sauce 22
ají criollo 12
ají de Huacatay 25
almonds: Mallorcan romescu sauce 81
anchovies: salsa verde piccante 71
Antillais caper and Scotch Bonnet sauce 56
Antillais fish marinade 57
apricot and almond chilli jam 37
aquavit: spiced conserva antica 76
avocados: classic guacamole 15

babari ko achar 113
baharat blend 82
barbecue baste 97
beef: chimichurri beef "al Asado" 26
  Korean chilli marinade for 130
Bengali kasundi 110–11
berbere paste 42
blachan 134
black beans: Caribbean black bean and mango salsa 61
  Hunan-style chilli and black bean sauce 145
blackening spice, Cajun 87
Bolivian Llajua hot sauce 24
boozy berry tirami-ifle 74
braii sauce 44
breads, naan 105
butter: chilli barbecue baste 97
  niter kibbeh 43
  spicy brown roux for gumbo 88

cabbage: kimchi 131
Cajun blackening spice 87
Cajun potato salad 90
capers: Antillais caper and Scotch Bonnet sauce 56
cardamom-infused apricot and almond chilli jam 37
Caribbean black bean and mango salsa 61

chermoula 31
  chermoula mackerel 32
chicken: jalfrezi curry 116
  Louisiana gumbo 90
  mussaman curry 124
  pinchitos morunos 73
  Szechuan chicken marinade 146
  traditional roast chicken in adobo mojado 64
chilli pickled ginger 151
chilli jam, cardamom-infused apricot and almond 37
chimichurri, Dan's favourite 23
chimichurri beef "al Asado" 26
Chinese cabbage: kimchi 131
Chinese curry sauce 147
Chinese pickled green chillies 142
chutney 112–13
cochinita pibil 16
coconut: blachan 134
  hot chilli coconut dip 62
  xacuti curry powder 108
conserva antica, spiced 76
coriander/cilantro: ají criollo 12
  Bolivian Llajua hot sauce 24
  chermoula 31
  pebre 24
crab, lime and Scotch Bonnet sauce 60
Creole rémoulade 86
curry: Chinese curry sauce 147
  jalfrezi curry 116
  Japanese curry powder 150
  lamb vindaloo 105
  Malay curry powder 135
  mussaman curry 124
  mussaman curry paste 123
  pinang kerrie sauce 45
  sour fish curry paste 107
  "sour orange" curry paste 127
  Sri Lankan dark roast curry paste 106
  Thai green curry paste 120
  Thai red curry paste 121

vindaloo curry paste 102
  xacuti curry powder 108

Dan's Caribbean classic 53
Dan's favourite chimichurri 23
Dan's roast tomato, garlic and Jalapeño ketchup 92–3
dips: classic guacamole 15
  hot and sweet chilli dipping sauce 96
  hot chilli coconut dip 62
  muhammara 83
  sabse borani 113
  Szechuan red and black dipping sauce 140

egusi sauce 48
Ethiopian berbere paste 42

fish: Antillais fish marinade 57
  Hunan chilli marinated fish 148
Fra Diavolo sauce 79
fruit: spiced conserva antica 76

ginger: chilli pickled ginger 151
  Japanese pickled ginger salad dressing 153
  rum, lime and ginger marinade 53
guacamole 15
gumbo: Louisiana gumbo 90
  spicy brown roux for 88

harissa paste 39
honey: green honey salsa 13
hot and sweet chilli dipping sauce 96
huacatay, ají de 25
Hunan chilli marinated fish 148
Hunan chilli sauce 143
Hunan-style chilli and black bean sauce 145

jalfrezi curry 116
jalfrezi paste 114
Japanese curry powder 150
Japanese pickled ginger salad dressing 153

Jordanian baharat blend 82

Kashmiri lamb marinade 115
ketchup, roast tomato, garlic and Jalapeño 92–3
kimchi 131
koftas, West African lamb 46
Korean chilli marinade for beef 130

La Kama spice blend 34
lamb: Kashmiri lamb marinade 115
  lamb vindaloo 105
  West African lamb koftas 46
lemon: seriously hot chilli and citrus marinade 54
limes: Antillais fish marinade 57
  crab, lime and Scotch Bonnet sauce 60
  rum, lime and ginger marinade 53
Louisiana gumbo 90
Louisiana spicy sauce 87

mackerel, chermoula 32
Malay curry powder 135
Mallorcan romescu sauce 81
mangoes: Caribbean black bean and mango salsa 61
  rum, lime and ginger marinade 53
marinades: Antillais fish 57
  Kashmiri lamb 115
  Korean chilli for beef 130
  Nepalese sekuwa 109
  for pinchitos morunos 73
  rum, lime and ginger 53
  seriously hot chilli and citrus 54
  sherry vinegar and smoked paprika 81
  simple orange and cumin 54
  Szechuan chicken 146
  teriyaki 153
  the ultimate peri-peri 40
mayonnaise: Creole rémoulade 86
Mediterranean seasoning rub 68

mint: ají de Huacatay 25
  babari ko achar 113
mole poblano 20–1
monkfish with grilled
  vegetable salad 58
"Moorish spikes" 73
Moroccan tagine paste 30
mostarda Mantovana 77
mother-in-law sauce 52
muhammara 83
mussaman curry 124
mussaman curry paste 123
mustard: Bengali kasundi
  110–11
  mostarda Mantovana 77

naan breads 105
nam prik pao 126
nasi goreng 136
nasi goreng spice paste 134
Nepalese onion chutney
  112
Nepalese sekuwa
  marinade 109
New Mexican green chilli
  sauce 95
niter kibbeh 43
noodles, teriyaki salmon
  with 154
North African rub 39
nuoc cham, Ho Chi Minh-
  style 128

oil, red chilli 140
onions: braii sauce 44
  lamb vindaloo 105
  pyaj ko achar 112
  red pickles 16
  roasted pepper and
    caramelized onion
    burger relish 98
  sabse borani 113
  sofrito 78
  spicy brown roux for
    gumbo 88
orange and cumin
  marinade 54

pak choi: kimchi 131
paprika: adobo mojado 64
  Mediterranean
    seasoning rub 68
  patatas bravas sauce 70
  sherry vinegar and
    smoked paprika
    marinade 81
parsley: chermoula 31
  Dan's favourite
    chimichurri 23
  salsa verde piccante 71
  the ultimate peri-peri
    marinade 40
patatas bravas sauce 70
peanut butter: tuong goi

cuon 129
peanuts: nasi goreng
  spice paste 134
  sambal kacang 133
  tsire powder 46
pebre 24
peppers (bell): braii sauce
  44
  egusi sauce 48
  Fra Diavolo sauce 79
  green honey salsa 13
  harissa paste 39
  hot and sweet chilli
    dipping sauce 96
  jalfrezi curry 116
  Louisiana spicy sauce
    87
  Moroccan tagine paste
    30
  muhammara 83
  roasted pepper and
    caramelized onion
    burger relish 98
  rouille 68
  sofrito 78
  spicy brown roux for
    gumbo 88
peri-peri marinade 40
pickles: chilli pickled
  ginger 151
  Chinese pickled green
    chillies 142
  Japanese pickled ginger
    salad dressing 153
  kimchi 131
  red pickles 16
pili-pili sauce 48
pinang kerrie sauce 45
pinchitos morunos 73
  marinade for 73
pineapple: mussaman
  curry 124
pork: cochinita pibil 16
potatoes: Cajun potato
  salad 90
  mussaman curry 124
prawns/shrimp: nasi
  goreng 136
Prime Minister Errol
  Barrow's hot chilli sauce
  63
pumpkin seeds: egusi
  sauce 48
pyaj ko achar 112

quinces: mostarda
  Mantovana 77

ras el hanout spice blend
  35
  classic North African
    rub 39
recado rojo 19
red chilli oil 140

relishes: Bengali kasundi
  110–11
  roasted pepper and
    caramelized onion
    burger relish 98
rémoulade, Creole 86
rice: nasi goreng 136
romescu sauce 81
rosemary and chilli-
  infused vinegar 69
rouille 68
rubs: classic North
  African rub 39
  Mediterranean
    seasoning rub 68
rum, lime and ginger
  marinade 53

sabse borani 113
salads: Cajun potato salad
  90
  crunchy salad 154
  grilled vegetable salad
    58
  spinach and preserved
    lemon salad 32
salmon, teriyaki 154
salsas: ají criollo 12
  Caribbean black bean
    and mango 61
  green honey 13
  salsa roja 15
  salsa verde piccante 71
salt: classic North African
  rub 39
sambals 132–3
sambar powder 103
seafood sauce, zesty
  Cajun 89
sekuwa marinade,
  Nepalese 109
seriously hot chilli and
  citrus marinade 54
sesame seeds: za'atar
  spice blend 82
sherry vinegar and
  smoked paprika
  marinade 81
Simon's kasundi 110
sofrito 78
sour fish curry paste 107
"sour orange" curry paste
  127
South African braii sauce
  44
Spanish seasoning paste 70
spinach: sabse borani 113
Sri Lankan dark roast
  curry paste 106
Szechuan chicken
  marinade 146
Szechuan chilli paste 144
Szechuan red and black
  dipping sauce 140

tagine paste, Moroccan 30
tahini: walnut, sesame
  and chilli dressing 36
teriyaki marinade 153
teriyaki salmon 154
Texas-style hot green
  chilli sauce 95
Thai green curry paste 120
Thai red curry paste 121
tirami-ifle, boozy berry 74
tomatillos: Texas-style hot
  green chilli sauce 95
tomatoes: Bolivian Llajua
  hot sauce 24
  braii sauce 44
  Dan's roast tomato,
    garlic and Jalapeño
    ketchup 92–3
  egusi sauce 48
  lamb vindaloo 105
  Louisiana spicy sauce 87
  Mallorcan romescu
    sauce 81
  mole poblano 20–1
  Moroccan tagine paste
    30
  patatas bravas sauce 70
  roast tomato and
    chipotle hot sauce 18
  roast tomato sauce 92
  salsa roja 15
  sofrito 78
tsire powder 46
tuong goi cuon 129

Vietnamese peanut sauce
  129
vindaloo curry paste 102
  lamb vindaloo 105
vinegar: rosemary and
  chilli-infused vinegar
  69
  sherry vinegar and
    smoked paprika
    marinade 81

walnuts: muhammara 83
  walnut, sesame and
    chilli dressing 36
West African lamb koftas
  46

xacuti curry powder 108

yogurt: babari ko achar
  113
  Kashmiri lamb marinade
    115
  Nepalese sekuwa
    marinade 109
  sabse borani 113
Yucatecan achiote paste 19

za'atar spice blend 82

Acknowledgments

When I wrote this for "The Red Hot Chilli Cookbook" I utterly failed to mention a great many people without whom the whole project would have been a disaster – so this time I am apologizing in advance to those I forget.

Becky, Freddie, Theo, Ella and Monty for accepting that they have a slightly distracted husband and father, and encouraging me to carry on anyway. Sam, who despite working with me for 6 years unbelievably still supports these "new ideas". My editor Céline for patiently dealing with all the headaches my sporadic way of working creates without shouting at me once. Colin and Linda for not complaining that every meal contains chilli. Owen and Michelle, Patrick and Katharina, Tim and Athene, Geoff and Liz, Anna, Chris and Rachael, Tony and Linda, Jamie and all their children for being the people who I love to experiment on. Cindy, Julia, Leslie, Lauren and everyone else at RPS who again made this fun! Peter and Lizzy for (again) making my recipes look stunning. And a few people who inspired me to write about food: Elizabeth David, Keith Floyd, Rick Stein, Simon Majumdar, Hugh F-W, Kenny Atkinson, and finally my Mum who, despite everything, ensured I knew how to cook and my Dad who always ate everything I made for him.